REACH FOR THE SKY

Do Ros agus Camille le

smuointe ó gCuinemara i nÉirinn. Iúil '78

Thank ye for the laughs and spirit you left

behind with us in Ireland .... fond memories

always.   Enjoy the read

Cú Ó Muircheartaigh.

REACH FOR THE SKY

Pat Falvey

with Dan Collins

THE COLLINS PRESS

Every effort has been made to contact individuals, authors and publishers whose work has been quoted. The publishers wish to apologise for any errors or omissions and would be grateful to be notified of any corrections that should be incorporated into the next edition of the book.

Published by The Collins Press, Carey's Lane, The Huguenot Quarter, Cork

© Text and photographs Pat Falvey, 1997

For motivational and Management lectures, guided exploration and expeditions, Ireland and world-wide, contact
Pat Falvey, Global Adventures, 367 Blarney Street, Cork, Ireland
Tel/fax: +353 (0) 21 303133
Mobile: +353 (0) 88 540204
E-mail: (1) patfalvey@tinet.i.e.

Printed in Ireland by Colour Books Ltd., Dublin

Jacket design by Upper Case Ltd., Cornmarket Street, Cork

ISBN: 1-898256-32-2

ACKNOWLEDGEMENTS

I would like to pay special thanks to all my team mates and everybody around the world who encouraged and supported me until the completion of my Seven Summits.

A special thanks is due to Dan Collins for his professional help and encouragement.

I want to thank my many sponsors for their belief and financial support.

Finally, I owe a great debt to my family for their patience and understanding, in particular to Marie, Brian, Patrick, Mum and Dad, and my brothers and sisters.

CONTENTS

*To my family, friends and loyal supporters
and all who, in the course of their lives,
follow their dreams
and endeavour to make them a reality*

INTRODUCTION

Dream and dream big. But remember son, it's in trying to make your dreams a reality that the success lies. Achieving the goals set by your dreams are a bonus.

Tim Falvey: my father

Throughout the course of our lives we are faced with many challenges. We set goals and ambitions and try to achieve them. To each person the dream is different. However, when we succeed in making our dreams a reality, the sense of achievement we all feel is the same.

My dream and ambition was once to become a millionaire, later to climb Everest and at a later stage again to climb the highest mountain on each of the seven continents in the world. This became an adventure through the most remote places on earth, discovering the traditions and cultures of the peoples I visited and lived with.

Over the centuries people have set out to explore and conquer, to get to some place, raise a flag as the first to triumph and ensure fame. It's in the nature of man – to challenge, to succeed, to dream and endeavour to make the dreams a reality.

I left school at the early age of 15 to become a millionaire. I was a workaholic with only one focus in life – to achieve my dream which I did by the age of 26. However, by the time I was 29 I was facing financial ruin, my dream and life were shattered and I was broke. From the depression of failure I reassessed my lifestyle and objectives in life. After spending two days on the Irish hills, a new dream took hold – to climb to the highest point on our planet.

My new ambition, to climb Mount Everest, gave my life a new sense of purpose and an objective to strive towards. On the way, I would achieve a lot of smaller successes which would give me the opportunity to rebuild my lost confidence and self-esteem. This became a turning point in my life and took me on a new course of high adventure. On occasions I had to live in tents for up to 70 days at a time, without any modern comforts. I gained a new appreciation for life, when I'd return from my expeditions after living in primitive conditions with simple people (that I fell in love with). I found myself enjoying the simple things in life a lot more, like putting my finger on a light switch and a bulb would light, turning on a shower and getting hot water.

Along the way I was able to take lessons that I had learned in my early years and turn them to my advantage. I remembered my maternal grandmother, who could neither read nor write, but was a great businesswoman and sold second hand clothes in open markets around the country for a living, to support her family. Her advice and philosophy that she drummed into me as a child was, 'If you think you can, you will. If you think you can't, you won't.' So if you set your mind on something always believe you can do it.

My father was not formally educated, though he taught me the importance of common sense. I will always remember his counsel when I sat down and cried. I was 18 years of age. Frustrated and depressed, I worried that I had made a mistake in following my dream to become a millionaire. 'Son, you're streetwise and clever and you're also a dreamer. So, dream and dream big. But remember son, it's in trying to make your dreams a reality that the success lies. Achieving the goals set by your dreams are a bonus.' I have used his counsel on many occasions in my business and adventure life.

Since those early days I have made the million (and lost it), and I have stood on the highest point on seven continents. I have had great adventures and made my dreams a reality. While achieving this I have learnt an enormous amount about life itself. To enjoy getting on top of any summit you have to start in the valley. Our lives are like the mountains – a series of high and low points that make up successes and failures.

I have made friends all over the world. I have lived with people of different cultures and traditions. I have learnt how similar they are to us. They love, hate, care. They feel sorrow, pain, joy and most importantly they strive for improvement and success just like all of us. I've become opinionated on many issues, having taken a special interest in our environment and the destruction of ethnic tribes and cultures around the world.

However, whenever I think of my career to date as a businessman and adventurer, nothing will ever compare with the emotion and enjoyment I felt as I stood on the summit of Mount Everest at

9.10am on 27 May 1995, with tears running down my face and adrenalin flowing – a sacred patch of ground six miles high in the sky. I clinched my fists tight, bent my elbow and swung my hand in the thin air with excitement as I roared emotionally, 'Yes, I've done it. I'm on top of the world.' I fell to my knees and prayed for a safe return.

I then thought of how Mount Everest in the twentieth century has become one of the ultimate symbols of human endeavour. Its name today is a household word and represents the world's highest mountain. It is also used as the metaphor for the goals and challenges that people set themselves. The trials and tribulations involved here are applicable to the challenges every one of us faces in our daily lives – whether it's a student passing an exam; a person getting the job they want so badly; conquering a serious illness; or a business person, clinching that long sought after deal that they worked so hard to put together. The person's adrenalin is flowing, their emotions are running high and they are proud of the achievement. They clinch their fist tight, raise it high in the air and say, 'yes, I've done it'. That is their Everest. That is every bit as exciting to them as I felt when I stood on the highest point on earth.

I invite you to read my story. It's of a dreamer that followed his dreams and made them a reality.

In the Footsteps of Dead Men

Before leaving, I climb the mountain.
High among sheep and bladed winds,
I add my stone to the peak's cairn,
And another for you: a summit reached.

Sean Dunne

Walking in the footsteps of dead men can cause uneasiness, especially above 8,000 metres (26,000 feet), a height at which man's fragility becomes all too apparent. Mount Everest, which to the Tibetan people is known as Chomolungma, 'Goddess, Mother of the Earth', can be a forbidding place. At just under 700 metres from the summit of the mountain, it is minus 30 degrees Celsius and I'm sitting in my tent feeling cold, hungry, exhausted but, at the same time, oddly exhilarated.

The only thing separating me from the direct extremes of weather, which seem to radiate with fury from the core of this inspiring and intimidating region, is a thin skin of man-made material – my tent. I am trying hard to concentrate on the final stages of the climb ahead. Unflinching resolve to get to the top is needed through many more long hours of punishing, snail-pace hard work.

There is no easy way to climb Everest. Some mountaineers have taken routes other than the North-Northeast Ridge. Others have stacked the odds even higher by climbing without oxygen. Whatever you choose, it is still seventy days of severe effort to reach that sacred pinnacle six miles high. Many brave men and women, native Sherpas from Tibet, Nepal and China and non-native adventurers, have given their lives back to the 'Mother of the Earth'.

In 1924, British mountaineers George Mallory and Andrew Irvine suffered the same extremes of temperature and felt the same aches in their muscles and joints. They too were spurred-on by the identical inner forces which have brought me here to make my second attempt to scale the most alluring of mountains, above which there is only sky. Tragically, those two pioneering climbers were

15

lost on the icy slopes just above our camp. When only a few hundred feet from the summit the men were last sighted, through a break in the clouds, by their colleagues camped high on the flanks of the mountain's dark side. I will take their memory and that of all others who have sacrificed their lives to Chomolungma, to the summit.

Reaching the top is just half the accomplishment – getting back can be every bit as demanding and dangerous a task. You have not conquered this, or any other mountain, until you have returned from the peak to the starting point, safely.

Australian James Allen, my climbing partner, and I were pushing for our first attempt, days earlier, on the summit when, at 7,900 metres, Chomolungma spoke to us. Her words were not welcoming. Her message came via jetstream winds which, at lesser altitude, would leave a swath of destruction in their path.

Our tent at 7,900 metres (25,900 feet) on Everest. One of the scariest times of my life as we feared being blown off.

16

For two days we lay huddled inside our cramped, flimsy tent pitched precariously on a terrifyingly exposed rocky outcrop on the icy North Face as the voice of the mountain roared and screamed with a demonic intensity. The force of the wind, which was lashing down on us in excess of 100 miles per hour, pushed the thin cocoon of tent against our helpless bodies as we lay in wait for some respite. We both knew that even if the tent withstood the onslaught indefinitely, our bodies could not. At this height we were burning up 6,000 calories each day while our rations merely replaced one-sixth of this life force. Here, the oxygen in the air was one-third that at sea level. Even breathing ceased to become a simple and natural function. At this elevation, man begins to expire, slowly and surely.

The physical complications caused by lack of oxygen are myriad and all too often fatal. In 1993, my first attempt on Everest provided much disturbing evidence of man's frailty in extreme conditions. On that occasion I was driven away from the summit by those same winds which can become an impenetrable barrier. Others in my team were not so fortunate and were sadly denied the opportunity to return to Everest. Dr Karl Heinze, a friend on that first expedition, died of a high altitude disorder and was buried in an icy grave on the mountain. Heinze, a NASA scientist and Shuttle astronaut, had been carrying out geological experiments at high altitude when struck down by acute high altitude sickness.

In 1994, the previous year, six people stood atop Everest. Of those, only four returned. Among the dead was a climbing associate, Mick Rheinberger, who perished on the very slope just beyond where we now lay pinned-down by a force no mortal being could ignore.

Since the first western expedition to Everest was inaugurated in 1921, fewer than 600 climbers have stood on top of the world. And, as I write this, the death toll exceeds 140. Courageous men and women who have made the ultimate sacrifice in their struggle to briefly claim that sacred patch of ground – the pinnacle of Chomolungma.

I know now that one of the properties vital in mountaineering is in fact crucial to our survival in all walks of life. This is the ability to recognise when it is time to retreat. My father once revealed this pearl of wisdom to me when, as a child, I came under the glare

James Allen, my partner on Everest in 1995, from Australia.

of neighbourhood bullies. 'Hit and run, Pat. Hit and run', was his no-nonsense advice. The value of those words remains precious as I lie here, many years later, in this evocative place.

We had weighed up the situation and decided, at this juncture, that dropping down made more sense than going up. Our determination was to survive this skirmish with Mother Nature and return to fight another day.

'James, would you bring my car around to the front. I think it's time we were going,' I quipped. Shortly after leaving this bivouac, the tent was ripped to shreds by the unmerciful winds. Angry and frustrated, we felt we had lost the opportunity to achieve our goal.

On 26 May, 1995, James and I returned to the team's highest camp, at 8,200 metres, having spent four days recovering in Advance Base Camp at 6,100 metres from our first unsuccessful assault.

On arrival there we were surprised to encounter another member of our expedition, Andre Tremouliere, a team mate from France. He was in our tent, exhausted, cold and sucking sweet oxygen from a bottle. He was very upset and crying uncontrollably. He did not want to leave his sleeping bag and had no desire to either go up or down the mountain. He had retreated back to High Camp earlier that day because he thought he had suffered a minor heart attack while climbing in the cold, exposed rock of the Yellow Band, a few hundred metres above where we were now precariously camped.

It was difficult to convince this spiritually and physically broken man that he could not stay above 8,000 metres, not in such a

18

weakened condition. One hour of gentle persuasion later and Andre was heading off down the mountain to Advance Base Camp where he would later make a full recovery. He bade a sad farewell and slowly descended, clutching a bottle of oxygen as a child would a favourite toy.

Later we were joined by another team mate, Bob Hemstead, a tough North American who when not climbing worked in the Alaskan oil fields.

Shoe-horned into a small two-man tent we boiled water and devoured a meal of dehydrated carbohydrates which had the look and consistency of baby food. Bob was on his way back to base having been involved in an almost fatal accident. When just 50 metres from the top of the mountain he slipped and fell helplessly down a steep slope before coming to a miraculous halt on an outcrop of rock, face down into the huge gully known as the Great Northern couloir. As he clung upside down to the rock, two of the summit team that day, Greg Child, a professional climber and writer from Seattle, and Sherpa Angbabu, hastily knotted together what few pieces of rope they had to throw Hemstead a life-line. He fastened this around his waist and was pulled to safety back up the slope just below the roof of the world. He fractured his hip in the fall but eventually made it to the summit where the Alaskan cowboy performed a rope trick, one not nearly as dramatic as that which had earlier saved him from certain death.

For twelve long, agonising hours that day we gasped and waited for a break in the weather. Time, provisions and resolve were fast running out. If I only had had a comfortable sleeping bag with which to cocoon myself I felt it might be more bearable. But I had none. Neither had my companions. Before this stage we had jettisoned all extra weight thinking that our goal was well within reach. Sleeping bags were considered superfluous. All we allowed ourselves was the clothing we wore – thermal underwear made up the first layer, then a full down suit and an outer jacket and overtrousers made from specially developed all-weather, lightweight fabrics.

My boots were technically advanced climbing footwear manufactured from a high tensile synthetic rubber called Neoprene and insulated with the same material NASA used in their space shuttles. Over these I wore gaiters to prevent snow getting inside the boot and, where necessary, strapped crampons on the sole and heel for traction on ice. Strapped to my waist I carried a Pentax 105 and Canon 100 camera determined that should one fail the other might provide the ultimate holiday snaps. So much had changed since the 1920s when the first westerners picked up the gauntlet to the greatest climbing challenge.

Among the general equipment carried by the successful Hillary-Tenzing expedition which on 29 May, 1953, made world news, were Shetland pullovers, string vests, woollen underwear, cigarettes and pipe tobacco, pressure cookers and alarm clocks. The boots worn by the first Everest conquerors – Hillary took size 12 and Tenzing size six – were described at the time as being of 'revolutionary design'. But, despite the great effort made by the manufacturer, the kapok, fibre-insulated footwear developed splits through which snow entered.

But I felt no smugness because of the superiority of our modern climbing equipment. The struggle between man and mountain has not been lessened by advances in manufacturing and through the discovery of synthetic, lightweight and durable materials. The gear may have changed over the decades but the game has not. In the words of John Hunt, who was so much part of the Hillary-Tenzing achievement, 'this tussle between men and a mountain reaches beyond the scope of mountain climbing in its physical aspect. It seems to me to symbolise man's struggle to come to terms with the forces of nature; it speaks eloquently of the continuity of this struggle and of the bond between all those who have taken part in it.'

For us the element of the unknown had been diffused by the first brave men to enter Everest's domain. But, singly or together, weather and altitude still held awesome powers which, if unleashed upon us, could create situations of unique and unprecedented ferocity. We reckoned that on a final assault, if the weather granted us such an honour, our rucksacks should contain no more than two bottles of vital, life-supporting oxygen; two litres of a water, salts and concentrated carbohydrate solution and nothing else.

As the hours wore on there was little to lift my spirits. Meal time became monotonous. Everything we had to eat was dehydrated and concentrated, or both. Breakfast tasted just like lunch which, in turn, tasted just like dinner which, frustratingly, tasted just like dessert. But, a few cans of stew or fruit could, at this altitude, have tipped the scales against our physical ability to make camp at this height. Scientists have calculated that a twenty pounds load at 6,000 metres (20,000 feet approximately), is equivalent to carrying a man, or woman, your own exact size up a flight of steps.

My digestive system groaned angry protestations, having been denied square, interesting meals for too long. Outside the tent the snow-laden wind kept up a constant, eerie wailing.

Imagination can be a curse in situations like these. Half in and half out of sleep I sometimes imagined I could hear voices carried on the wind. Thoughts of Mallory and Irving, more than the other mountaineers who had perished on Everest, would flood my mind. I could not help but dwell on the fact that James, at twenty-two, was the same age as Irving and I the same age as Mallory, thirty-eight, when they headed off on their third and last Everest adventure. There were times when I questioned the rationale behind man's desire to risk his very life for twenty minutes or so, of personal glory on the top of the world.

You don't spend long months, even years in many cases, organising costly Everest expeditions and then, once you get there, the best part of eight or more weeks walking, climbing, struggling and crawling to its summit just 'because it's there'. When Mallory uttered those oft-quoted words I feel what he was really trying to say was, if you have never combined the forces of body and soul to undertake a seemingly impossible task, how could I explain why some men, and women, must pit themselves against the extremes of their own environment. Sherpas believe that there is a spiritual umbilical chord which, no matter how far they stray from home, will draw them back to their lofty Himalayan hamlets. And, maybe this same unearthly attraction to the mountains can dwell within people other than Sherpas.

The thoughts in my head went through some mental blender as I waited in the tent – thoughts of home, triumph, failure and the threat of frostbite, rockfall, avalanche or slipping on the long, exposed traverse that hung above us. I felt as if the goblins and ghosts of Everest were playing with my sanity and beckoning me to the top. A myriad of memories flashed through my muddled mind. These were the twelve longest, most agonising hours of my life – a half day of hell on earth as we discussed our next move.

On Friday, 26 May, 1995 two months into the expedition, the

hand radio crackled to the familiar tone of Mike Smith, whose tent was pitched adjacent to us at the last camp before the summit.

'Come in Pat, come in James.' I hastily acknowledged the call. The news was not good. The temperature was dropping and the wind was continuing to grow in intensity. But, both he and his climbing partner Brigitte Muir, a 36 year-old Australian going for the last of her seven summits, had decided to launch a final assault on the peak.

Both James and I immediately felt a rush of emotion and adren-alin. The disappointment of last week's effort, the freezing cold, the awful food and the constant, battering-ram winds could no longer dampen our enthusiasm. I looked at James – he stared back. I put my thumbs up – he did likewise. Simultaneously our faces broke into a smile as I picked up the radio and, with a tremor in my voice, seeing my determination mirrored in James' wide-eyed expression, said, 'Come in Mike. We're going for it. What do you and Brigitte intend doing?'

There was a slight pause. 'We're going too.'

The decision had been taken. Nothing could stop us now. Our determination had reached a spiritual intensity far greater than any wind which lashed this snow and ice-covered temptress to so many brave and determined climbers.

In the dead of night, with the thermometer in our tent reading minus 35 degrees Celsius, we made ready our equipment and rations for the final onslaught as the words of a popular Irish folk song rang in my head.

> *You may travel far, far*
> *From your own native home,*
> *Far away o'er the mountains ...*

THE HARD WAY UP

Then draw upon strength
And formulate a plan
And every time you think you can't
Remember that you can.

Bruce B. Wilmer

Mary B O'Callaghan was known to one and all as Mary B. She was my maternal grandmother and a distinct focal point in my early childhood. I was born in 1957, the same year the United States of America, despite its advanced technology, received a jolting kick in the pants when the USSR's Sputnik 1 became the first satellite sent into orbit.

At home, in Cork, the dawning of the Space Age aroused little curiosity. In that unique Cork way of looking at the 'big picture', some already blamed 'them things they're sending into space' for causing inclement weather.

In the 1950s Cork was a vibrant place. Major motor, tyre and textiles factories brought about an employment revolution in the harbour city. People had disposable income, though not much. Houses, which a generation earlier differed little from basic rural homesteads by way of conveniences, now boasted indoor toilets and maybe even a plumbed bath for use on Saturday nights.

I was the first child born to Tim and Abina and we lived on Baker's Road in the working class northside suburb of Gurranebraher. My dad, like his father before him, was a bricklayer and stone mason. Like most people in the neighbourhood, he worked hard for a living – damn hard. We lived in an area where out of some 4,000 homes only three were privately owned – the remainder being local authority houses.

As the demand for new housing grew and Cork went through a construction surge, Tim realised he could make a better living by becoming a sub-contractor to the larger building firms. He had no working capital and only the basic skills of masonry, but he used his inherent charm and sheer single-mindedness to pave his way to success in both business and later, in politics. But the ladder to

Tim's goal had a few unstable rungs – as the family would later discover.

I never knew my paternal grandmother. She died before middle age, having given birth to fourteen children. Five died in infancy, something which caused her deep grief and hurt.

Of the nine surviving children, there were eight boys and one girl, Mary, who took on the responsibility of running the household after her mother's death. All the lads worked in the building line. Some of them became bricklayers of legendary ability, especially a dark, handsome strapping man named Paddy.

The only thing Paddy did better and faster than lay blocks was sink pints of black stout. He was known as 'The Blacker', as was his father before him. This was either a reference to his dark hair and sallow skin or his fondness for black stout – probably a combination of the two.

All the Falvey boys, my father included, enjoyed the hard work, hard drinking life of the 'brickies'. Later, Paddy's death as a shrunken, wasted and cancerous alcoholic made me resolutely determined not to take on the mantle of 'The Blacker' Falvey.

'Jesus, that poor man. God save us all,' Mary B would say, as she sorted through piles of second-hand clothes. These she sold from a stall in the city centre. It was November 1963 and US President John F Kennedy had just been assassinated in Dallas.

Mary B couldn't read or write but the news of Kennedy's death had spread by word of mouth to everyone in Gurranebraher. The image of the President shared the same picture frame with Pope John XXIII above many kitchen mantelpieces and he had been held in God-like esteem by the Irish. He was, after all, 'one of our own'. The previous June, Kennedy had visited Cork during his ecstasy-inducing Irish tour. The memory of his fresh and smiling face remained with the people of Cork, now in collective mourning.

'That poor young woman, God love her,' Mary B said of Kennedy's widow.

Mary knew what it was like to lose a husband. With six small children she had found herself socially stranded and alone when her husband walked out of their small council house in Orrery Road and never came back. Her survival instinct was more powerful than the initial feeling of hopelessness and resignation when she became a young, deserted mother. But her survival instinct was strong.

Mary B entered the rag trade. On her donkey and butt, a simple two-wheeled cart, she became a familiar figure along the roads between the north side suburbs and the inner city Coal Quay where the 'carters' plied their trade daily from kerb-side stalls.

The summer President Kennedy visited Cork, my parents decided I should move in with Mary B as her family were now grown-up and gone. So, at six years of age, I became my grandmother's companion and her apprentice 'carter'. My memory of her is that of a small, physically strong woman that enjoyed life with a passion. And as a second hand clothes seller she had a rare business acumen.

Mary B O'Callaghan, my grandmother, who was an astute trader.

Three times a week my grandmother and three other traders would hire an open-back lorry and would load it up with big bundles of clothes and head to Macroom, Bandon and Mitchelstown where poorly paid farm labourers and often their miserly employers were her best customers. Mary B was more than a match for those who, when it came to paying, had the habit of putting their hand in their pocket and leaving it there.

On one occasion, in the West Cork town of Bandon, we were approached by a farmer of slight build. 'Look at the cut of this fellow, Pat. He has neither back, belly nor sides,' she muttered. 'Are you looking for trousers? I've just the pair.' Mary found the smallest waist size which she knew was, at least, two sizes too big.

Keeping up a constant banter, she talked him into trying them on over the pants he was wearing. He nervously placed his legs into the trousers as she pulled them up around his waist. She tied the flies and grabbed the back of the waist taking up the slack in her grip. She then hooked her index finger inside the tensioned

25

waist band at the front and convinced the man the trousers were 'made for him'. He agreed and the sale was made. She was a persuasive and assertive woman who was good at her job. Her work was her life and she loved it. She continued as a trader until she was taken ill at the age of 79.

My time spent with Mary B was both educational and exciting. After Mass each morning, a practice she reverently maintained until her death at the age of 81, Mary filled my days with hard, rewarding work. School took second place to trips to and from the Coal Quay where the city traders gathered. I carried my grandmother's bales of clothes in an old child's pram.

'I'll make a priest out of you yet,' she would tell me as I was marched, somewhat reluctantly, to the church each morning.

At twelve years of age, I was spending more time in my father's building yard and less time with Mary B. When Tim and Abina were approached by Mary with a view to having me enrolled in a seminary college, they undertook a serious review of the situation. My parents were devout Catholics but the priesthood was not in their plans for their eldest son. So my younger brother, Richard, became Mary B's new companion and I was destined to enter the building line once I finished my schooling.

Formal education was provided by the Christian Brothers at the North Monastery, a tough institution for boys known plainly and simply as 'The Mon'. I could never see the point in learning languages, mathematics, science or geography. I wanted to be a builder, not a damn 'know-it-all'. The Brothers were a bunch of men renowned for their fondness of applying the strap for failure to comply with their standards. They would never have tolerated my disinterest in lessons had it not been that outside of class I was a rising star in the Mon's athletics team.

I progressed as a runner from inter-schools' competitions to county, provincial and eventually All-Ireland success. I mixed well with the team and tried to conceal my insatiable and burning desire to win every competition I entered. Pushing myself to the limit was never enough. I always had to try and get one step beyond. Winning was not fuelled by the desire to beat everyone else. My only challenger was myself, my only ambition was that which I set for myself.

My dad shared my passion for athletics and I soon became aware of an unbreakable bond which has existed between us ever since. I looked forward to our weekends together when there was an athletics meeting to attend.

Training consisted of running along the roads in the neighbourhood a few evenings a week. This was sometimes marred by the taunts of local 'hard-chaws' who regarded my interest in sports as the mark of a 'shaper'. When one of my close running companions, Tom McKernan, was attacked with a knife and slashed across the face, I was summonsed as a witness. Some time later the assailant had his revenge when three of his hoodlum friends jumped me from behind and left me bruised and badly beaten. After recovering from a punctured lung, I was back in train-

Winning a race for the North Monastery at the age of 13.

ing when, again, I was confronted by the same street gang. With my father's advice to 'hit and run, Pat. Hit and run' echoing in my head, I grabbed a hurley wielded by one of the hooligans and hit him across the head. He dropped like a stone, unconscious.

'Christ almighty,' I nervously uttered looking at the still body of the youth on the ground at my feet.

'Call the guards,' I heard somebody shout in the background, 'and get an ambulance.'

Frozen with fear and certain that I had killed the bastard, I just stood there with the 'murder' weapon in my hand. I really believed I 'was done for'. The prospect of years as a juvenile prisoner entered my mind.

An ambulance arrived after what seemed like a terrifying eternity. The nurse knelt before the boy and in an instant revived him. 'Oh! thank God – he's not dead,' I thought.

'You'll be alright. Hurt yourself hurling, did you?' the nurse said to her still punch-drunk patient. 'You're just a little concussed

– you'll be fine in a while.'

'What happened here?' said a deep, bass voice. I turned to discover a member of the Garda Siochana towering over me. With faltering voice I gave him a blow-by-blow account of the encounter as he took copious notes.

'Off you go home now, boy. You'll be hearing from me. And the rest of you ... clear-off,' instructed the voice of authority.

For days afterwards I expected every knock on our door was that of the Gardaí (police), coming to take me away to jail. But, they never called and must have adopted the attitude that the fellow I had 'clocked' had it coming. I felt no pride resorting to violence that day but after that incident I was never bothered by street gangs again. I had earned respect, the hard way.

SERVING MY TIME

*If one advances confidently in the directions of his dreams and endeav-
ours to live the life he had imagined, he will meet with success
unexpected.*

Henry David Thoreau

In 1971, I left school without bothering to sit for my Intermediate
Examinations. The first pocket calculator had just been launched
on the market but I needed no such gizmos to ascertain how much
money I could earn as a block layer. So, I learned the skill as an
apprentice to my uncle, 'The Blacker' and my father's older brother Donie, who was also known as the 'Big Fella' because of his size.

Shortly before I walked through the gates of The Mon for the
last time, I was called to the headmaster's office. I knew why I had
been summoned and it came as no surprise. A day earlier, I had
been in class sitting at my desk doodling and paying no heed to the
lesson being delivered by our biology teacher. Recognising my
lapse in concentration, he suddenly let fly with the blackboard
duster, which whizzed past my head in a cloud of chalk dust.

'Wake up Falvey, this is a classroom not a bedroom,' he roared,
while the rest of the class broke into a fit of collective giggling.

Revenge would be mine, I decided. I was not going to be
exposed to ridicule and take it lying down.

A couple of weeks earlier, the class had been on a field trip and
had collected frog spawn which was kept in a tank at the back of
the class. Before leaving the school that day, I crept into the biology class and poured a bottle of sulphuric acid into the tank.
Needless to say, the tadpoles did not make it to the frog stage. Of
course this was a stupid, brainless thing to do but nonetheless typical of how a young schoolboy would illustrate the point that for
every person wishing to teach there are at least fifty not wanting to
be taught.

It was now time to face the less than mellifluous music of the
headmaster. With more than a little trepidation I knocked on the
heavy pine door. 'Tar isteach,' (Come in) said the stern voice of
Brother Keating.

Sitting behind his desk he looked the very epitome of what the Christian Brothers stood for – tough, hard working, no-nonsense educationalists.

'Conas tá tú?' (How are you?) he said, without looking up.

'Ceart go léoir bráthair,' (OK Brother).

He finished reading, then stood up, adjusted the thick leather belt which tied his almost threadbare black cassock at the waist and looked out his window, headmaster of all he surveyed.

'How's your father, Pat? Is he busy?'

'He's kept going, Brother,' I meekly replied.

'And your mother, I hope she's well also?'

'She couldn't be better, Brother.'

'The same couldn't be said of you, Pat. I think you could be better. Better behaved.' Here it comes, I thought. Will it be the strap, the cane or worse? 'It's been brought to my attention Pat that you may have poured sulphuric acid into the tadpole tank in the science room,' he said, looking down at his hard black leather shoes. 'Did you do it?'

I knew by now that Brother Keating never called you to his office over matters such as this unless he already knew all the facts. He was seeking affirmation, not confirmation. Admission of guilt could have dire consequences, a denial even more so.

'Yes, Brother,' I said dejectedly.

He turned from the window, came towards me, sat on the edge of his desk and stifled a chuckle. 'Will you be staying on after the Inter?'

'No, Brother. I'm going to work with my dad.'

'You'll be leaving us next year so, but I still have to punish you for that misguided experiment of yours.' Again, I'm sure I detected laughter being damped down within his sturdy frame. 'You'll be missed from the athletics team whatever about the science class.'

Fearful of my parents being told of my misdeeds and facing the disgrace of being expelled, tears welled in my eyes. He asked me if I enjoyed school. I timidly replied – 'No, Brother.'

He then cast judgement in the oddest and most unexpected fashion. The reprove I was to receive could not have been more unexpected and would change my outlook on life forever. Just as I was about to leave the room, Brother Keating went back to his position looking out of the window and said, 'fan noimead!'(wait a minute). After a brief pause, he placed his hand on my shoulder, looked at me fixedly in the eye and said – 'Pat, I'm not going to expel you, but you have to promise me one thing.'

'Yes Brother,' I replied, relieved and not sure what was coming next.

'I want you to tell yourself every day that no matter what it is you are doing, whether it is English, Irish or any other subject that "I am enjoying doing it", OK Pat?'

Not believing what my punishment was and thinking that Brother Keating must be cracking up, I immediately gave my answer. 'Yes Brother.'

'Go on, you caffler, back to your work.'

Every day for the next six months Brother Keating went out of his way to meet me and ask, 'well Pat, are you enjoying yourself today?'

To this I would automatically respond – 'Oh! yes Brother.'

Eventually, this mantra took hold of my conscious mind and I really did begin to enjoy studying subjects which previously I had abhorred. Out of school and in the workplace, I found Brother Keating's counsel easy to apply and keep me focused on the bright side of life.

My dad's business had gone from strength to strength but, cruelly, Tim took a fall. He had little capital put aside. The money he made was ploughed straight back into the firm. So, when a developer for whom my dad was carrying out a £500,000 contract went belly-up, the business took the full force of the collapse. Like hungry wolves, Falvey creditors came with their demands. Even the men who worked on our gangs sought money owing to them with a panic-fuelled immediacy.

This was a situation Tim had never encountered before. This became the terminal point of a chain reaction which, while not of his making, had become his to deal with. Facing the threat of liquidation, my dad sought release from the pressures which mounted daily. To use that almost apologetic expression, he 'turned to drink', as if booze was some great oracle to be consulted only at times of extreme duress.

I had another year to go at school, or so I thought. One evening, while my dad was in the throes of his drinking binge, there came a loud knocking on our front door.

'Holy mother of God, who's making that racket?' said my

mother as she hurried to answer the call. Standing there was a man I recognised, a casual labourer who sometimes worked for Tim. He was unsteady on his feet. 'Is Tim at home?' he slurred with a strong, fetid smell of alcohol from his breath.

'He hasn't come home yet,' said my mother, knowing it would be much later that night before he returned home bearing the same malodorous mantle of the hard drinker.

'I want my fuckin' money *now*,' he angrily demanded. I stood behind my mother, frightened and helpless. Abina eventually convinced the threatening caller that she had no money to give him.

'Tell Tim I'll be back for what he owes me. I'll be fuckin' back.'

She closed the door, leaned her head against it and cried. I stood there in the hallway frozen by my inability to do or say anything to ease my mother's pain. The strain of rearing a young family – six children, including myself – with a largely absentee husband was starting to take its toll. That night, I solemnly swore that she would never again have to face such abuse. I decided there and then that I would leave school as soon as possible to start work as a block layer and become a millionaire before I was twenty. I now set myself a goal and I was hungry to achieve it.

I resented my father for placing the family in such a money-strapped situation. At the time I gave little consideration to the deep hurt and pain he was suffering because of trust he had placed in others, trust which was not returned. Later, I would learn these valuable though unpleasant lessons myself.

An insatiable hunger grew inside me to leave school and make my fortune. At 15 years of age I entered my father's firm and began planning ways in which to make the business more profitable. Under the tutelage of my master mason, 'The Blacker', I was soon earning more money on the building line than I knew what to do with. My determination and assertiveness was initially met with the slight of the hired hands.

My father must have thought I was a pretentious little bollocks. I was, but I got the job done and he needed all the help he could get. His drinking was excessive for about a year and a half. It's a period I have tried to erase from my mind. It was a time when our home life was disturbed, dysfunctional. Our family would have broken up had it not been for the iron-willed determination of my mother.

One night, and not for the first time, she asked me to go to the local pub and try to bring Tim home. This was a task I often under-took. Usually, he would totally ignore my pleas or give me some bland assurance that he would be home after 'just one more for the road'. On this occasion my mother accompanied me to Paddy Taylor's in Blackpool. It wasn't difficult to find Tim in the dimly lit, smoke-filled bar. He was always the central character in a group of boozers, probably because when he had drinking money he was never shy to spread his largess.

Tim was too drunk to be embarrassed by the sudden appear-ance among his sponging flatterers of his wife and son. With little resistance, we each took an arm and carried him from the bar and slowly, embarrassingly half-carried, half-dragged him along the steep, busy streets of Fair Hill to our home.

For some reason which I have never fully grasped, my father's heavy drinking ended that night. I think he realised, even through the fug of alcohol in his mind, that my mother had been subjected to enough hardship. As strong as her mothering instincts were, I think my dad realised then that he had taken Abina's resolve too much for granted.

From that day on, Tim and I worked together with all the internecine friction of a father and son partnership. We fought a lot of the time and rarely agreed on how best to run a business. But, after the close of each working day we were a family united.

The company was getting back on the rails soon after Tim emerged from his lost eighteen months. Through sober determina-tion my dad fought hard to recoup his losses. At one point Tim, my uncles and some trusted employees, squatted round the clock for four weeks in a house owned by the developer who owed him money. My father believed that possession of property is nine-tenths of the law and if someone is trying to damage you or your family you fight back with all your powers to survive. Eventually, just before heading off to Britain, the insolvent developer cleared some, but not all, of the debt. Psychologically, more than fiscally, Tim felt vindicated.

By the time I was 16 years of age I had discarded the 'snot nosed brat' aura in the eyes of the men working for the firm. I now had full responsibility for twenty men, all of them older than me and Tim's imprimatur to issue 'walking papers' if I felt somebody was not pulling his weight.

Very often, my gang would be split up to work on separate projects. And, because it was my habit to keep each site under direct supervision, hopping from one to another in a chaotic but effective manner, I was known by the vainglorious title of 'The Galloping Major'. Despite this, I discovered an aptitude to relate to all my employees on an equal and fair footing while at the same time earning their respect as somebody who worked just as hard, if not harder, than anyone else.

In 1975, I became engaged to Marie Horgan, a quiet, gentle girl who lived in nearby Churchfield. We met through athletics when I was 14 and Marie two years older. I always pretended, until she accepted my proposal, to be older than her, rather than run the risk of rejection.

We set June 1977, my twentieth birthday, as the date of our wedding. While looking for a home, I became aware of a market opening to provide the economic momentum I needed to achieve millionaire status.

Must Not Quit

When things go wrong as they sometimes will,
When the road you're trudging seems all up-hill,
When the funds are low and the debts are high
And you want to smile, but you have to sigh,
When care is pressing you down a bit,
Rest if you must. But don't quit.

Nothing is as aggravating as calmness, or so it has often been said. But that's a notion I have never subscribed to. No matter what the situation I believe in keeping cool and composed. This doesn't come easy but it's a skill worth acquiring.

There are times however when the exception to the rule arrives on the scene, 'effing and blinding'. My father and I had agreed to pool our resources and work, as one, on my grand construction plan. Now here I was seated before a bank manager who had refused to accept Tim's application for a loan. The money was to be his stake in a project I was certain would not fail. While I had managed to get my father four square behind me, which was not an easy task, the bank manager was not so supportive.

'Pat, I've looked at the figures, the projections and I don't think it can work. I'm sorry, the answer is still no.'

My dream was being trod upon before my very eyes. The bank official's opinion was based on the fact that the company had recently suffered a set-back.

'Look at the figures again. It can't fail. Can't you see that?' I pleaded.

'Sorry, Pat. The element of risk is too great. Stay small and manageable, that's the best advice I can give you and your father,' said the small cog in a big machine, pretending to be otherwise.

Realising nothing would change his mind, I suddenly vented the frustration that had been welling up inside me.

'Fuck you so. I'll go somewhere else for a loan,' I said, rising quickly to my feet.

'Now, Mr Falvey. There's no need to use that kind of language. I'm only doing my job.'

Before he had the chance to say another word I was halfway out the door, pausing only briefly to inform him he was 'nothing but a bollocks'.

He took his revenge by withdrawing my father's overdraft facility at what was then a most inopportune time. Panic-stricken and not knowing what to do, we turned to our accountant. He in turn arranged a meeting with a progressive bank manager.

A few days later I was sitting before this manager of another bank discussing the same proposal. He looked at the figures I put before him, discussed them in some detail and declared that his bank would be happy to provide the loan and give my father any overdraft facility he needed.

So, with £12,000 capital, one-third raised by my dad, I began building houses for people like myself – newly-weds or those intending to get married on a tight budget. I figured couples needed basic housing, without the costly extras. I don't mean mud and wattle shacks but well-built, affordable, energy-efficient, comfortable dwellings which would not depreciate in time. The land on which the first houses were built was provided by a local businessman, Owen O'Callaghan. He was paid per site as each house was sold, an arrangement which was both harmonious and profitable for all concerned.

In June 1977, Marie and I married. It happened in spite of an earlier upset when £600, a considerable sum in those days, set aside for an engagement ring, was lost on shares which I thought were going to go through the roof but which instead went down the S-bend.

I was past my first year of trading and thirty-two 'starter' houses had been built and sold. For the next eight years the business flourished but as I approached my twenty-first birthday I realised my first million monetary goal was further down the road.

Marie and I had a very comfortable lifestyle and were expecting our first child, Brian. The business became the nucleus of my life. I gave no thought to holidays or any form of recreation. I could only derive pleasure from the success of the company. In the late 1970s the company, plus the worth of my investments, probably had a gross value of £1,000,000. My personal income was, even by today's standards, very rewarding. All profits went back into the company. There was no other way to maintain the momentum. My ambition to become a millionaire burned as intensely as when I first began working in my father's firm.

Pat Falvey (far right) as a prosperous businessman in the 1980s.

Trolling the market for potentially sound investments, I never stopped to consider that those who mistake their good luck for their merit are inevitably bound for disaster. I believed I had the Midas touch without even knowing who the fuck Midas was in the first place. Certainly, I had some good fortune but I also met some insatiable predators along the way.

The company was trading well. My father and I were major league builders, providing properties at both the upper and lower ends of the market.

In 1985, a recession which had swept across Europe began to have an influence on Irish commerce. I found myself with fingers in too many pies. These business interests were draining rather than supporting our construction company. The market began to collapse as increasing interest rates deterred prospective house purchasers. Our bank advised us of our over-traded position and suggested re-financing our companies. We struggled through 1985 against the ever-increasing recessionary undertow.

Early the following year, disaster loomed large on the horizon. With no prospect of an interest rate decrease it was obvious we could not achieve the sales goal necessary for our survival.

In April 1986, I was sitting in a pub with my dad, my brothers and a few of the lads working for us. The topic on everyone's lips was the horrific nuclear disaster at Chernobyl. But I cared little about the human tragedy which was unfolding and its environmental shock waves. My accountant had just focused my attention on more personal rather than global matters. Ireland was heading further into recession. The Central Bank, the last domino in the European monetary network, intended to increase loan interest rates even further.

By now, Marie and I had two boys, Brian and Patrick. We had been living, very comfortably, in an architect-designed, red brick house at Kerry Pike – an exclusive satellite of private homes between Cork city and Blarney. Suddenly I feared that we were about to lose everything, even our home.

Things reached a critical juncture just before the 1986 August Bank Holiday. Tim and I had spent long hours in discussion with bankers, accountants and our solicitor. At the end of these difficult deliberations, we agreed that our companies and investments were in a sorry state. We had not become totally immersed in this quagmire. There was still enough leeway to enable us to cease all trading and pay off our debtors. Both my dad and I agreed this was the only honourable thing to do.

I cried uncontrollably all that day. It was like all the light had been drained from my life. I felt alone, isolated and vulnerable. My only solace was that although seven building sites had closed today, the 220 men on our books were paid everything owing to them.

Driving home my mind was in turmoil. How could I explain to Marie and the boys that everything was gone, everything? I had found myself in the same position my father had been in when I was 14 years of age. I could not help but nervously wonder what effect this would have on my sons.

A song came on the car radio and in the back of my mind, I listened to the lines:

... and you may find yourself behind the wheel of a large automobile
And you may find yourself in a beautiful house, with a beautiful wife.
And you may ask yourself – well – how did I get here?

Pat with Marie, Patrick and Brian in the 1980s. It was Brian's anguish and my deep-rooted fear of failure which made me fight back.

I turned the car into our driveway and sat there for a long time not knowing how to break the news to my family. Little did I know that Marie had already read about our plight on the front page of the evening newspaper.

Conscious of family fears that we would have to sacrifice the house, I fought hard to ward off the feelings of surrender which possessed me. As best I could I explained to Brian, my eldest boy, that we might have to sell our home and move to the city, taking up residence in a local authority house. Brian, with tears streaming down his face, turned to me and said, 'But why, Dad. Why?' Being

39

a child, how could he understand?

A sense of failure welled up inside me but this was met by a growing determination to fight back and retain, at whatever cost, our house and home.

That night I sat in my living room alone. The family had gone to bed. My mother had called that evening. She felt I was getting too depressed by the whole situation or as she put it – 'too into yourself. It's not good for you.' Before leaving she took a folded page from her hand-bag and gave it to me. 'Here love, read that when you have a quiet moment.' I unfolded the page my mother had given me. It was a poem. Simple and to the point, I must have read it at least ten times that night and since then it has remained etched on my memory.

When things go wrong as they sometimes will,
When the road you're trudging seems all up-hill,
When the funds are low and the debts are high
And you want to smile, but you have to sigh,
When care is pressing you down a bit,
Rest if you must. But don't quit.

Life is queer with its twists and turns,
As every one of us sometimes learns,
And many a failure turns about
When he might have won had he stuck it out.
Don't give up though the pace seems slow –
You may succeed with another blow.

Success is failure turned inside out –
The silver tint of the clouds of doubt,
And you can never tell how close you are,
It may be near when it seems so far.
So, stick to the fight when you're hardest hit –
It's when things seem worst that you must not quit.

Must not quit, must not quit, must not quit. This sentiment ran through my mind like a train across a dark night.

I went to my office every morning after that and spent long days exploring every possible commercial avenue which might lead to financial stability. This placed me in some situations which had the potential to be riskier than many of my later exploits on the mountains.

On one occasion my search took me to Dublin where a budding entrepreneur opened a window on an exotic vista thousands of miles away. His proposal was to construct apartments using a radically-designed building block with integral insulation. The plan was to manufacture these blocks in a factory not far from the construction site of the apartments in the northern Egyptian port of Alexandria.

I got my dad interested in the scheme and we held the first meeting of many with an agent of the Egyptian government at the Burlington Hotel in Dublin. The agent was a suave, well-spoken Egyptian skilled in the ways of commerce. Our negotiations with him were crucial as nothing could be done without the imprimatur of his government.

We exhaustively discussed the blueprint with him. Finally we reached a preliminary agreement on the first phase of this £30 million project, the construction of the *insublock*-making factory. At home, we worked hard to secure tentative pledges for 10% financing. The agent had insisted that £3 million be placed in a special project account before work could begin. He remained evasive on one bothersome issue – *baksheesh.*

Enquiries to the Irish export agencies confirmed our worst fears. We would have to spend at least £3 million greasing the palms of the Egyptians from the agent down the baksheesh ladder to the bottom rung. Serious doubts set in before we were to sign the first contracts. Tim and I arrived in Dublin for the decision-day meeting.

It brings a smile to my face when I think of it now. Our businesses had collapsed but we were about to embark on a £30 million scheme without a penny in the bank, just a few uncertain pledges of financial support from business contacts. As Tim and I took the elevator to the hotel room for the critical meeting we could both sense each other's uneasiness.

'Pat, do you realise we have run-up a huge bill in this hotel over the past weeks. I don't even know how we're going to pay that and these Egyptians are expecting three million pounds in back-handers,' Tim said, with a distinct air of desperation.

'At least three million, it could be much more,' I replied, throwing fat on the fire. Our advisors had warned us the project could come to a standstill if this money was not provided. Wearing our

bravest faces, we entered the room. The agent sprang to his feet
and warmly welcomed us. I felt like somebody in a poker game
where the stakes had gone through the ceiling. We desperately
needed time out to reconsider our position. This was provided
when we discovered a crucial piece of documentation was missing
– the Egyptian government's declaration that their financial stake
was in place. The talks were suspended. The agent made some
frantic telephone calls from the next room and emerged apologetic
but confident.

'I am so sorry gentlemen for this minor inconvenience. My
banker's agent is on his way from Frankfurt with the document
you require. He should arrive at Dublin Airport in three hours'
time.'

In the meantime we decided we were not the big time players
we had hoped to become. The risk was too great. The worst case
scenario called for £3 million to be set aside for baksheesh which
my dad and I agreed was 'fuckin' crazy'.

The meeting reconvened three hours later and, sure enough,
here was the bank agent with proof positive of the Egyptian government's security. We could not have picked a more inopportune
moment to break the news that we were backing out of the deal.

'Surely you jest,' said the agent with the expression of a man
who had just had a very fine and valuable Persian rug pulled
unceremoniously out from under him. He cursed, threatened and
generally threw the most magnificent of Egyptian fits. But neither
my dad nor I gave a continental damn. Sitting there letting him
vent his spleen was, in effect, no skin off our noses. Had we
entered into the agreement we could have lost our heads financially, whatever about literally.

'What do we do now, Dad?' I asked Tim as we sat on the
Dublin-Cork train.

'Don't know, Pat. I just don't know.'

'Why don't we try pyramid selling. We could use our Egyptian
experience,' I joked.

'Good idea. Maybe the agent would like to come on board. But
first he has to pay me one million pounds *blacksleet* or whatever
they feckin' call it.'

We both laughed, realising you can be down but you can also
be down further still.

42

FAIR HILLS

Each chapter that is an ending
leads to a new beginning.
The past that we are leaving
means a future we are winning.

Bruce B. Wilmer

A banker is a person who lends you an umbrella when the weather is fine and takes it back when it begins to rain.

Late in the summer of 1986 I could sense the dull thud of the final nail being driven into my commercial coffin. The bank, which had earlier refinanced the business in a bid to keep it afloat, decided to unleash its lawyers who now came baying at my door. I had pledged my house as a guarantee against part of the bank loan, never suspecting that one day the re-possession of my family home would become a grim reality.

This was a period which left Marie and my eldest son Brian, who at the time was just old enough to grasp the gravity of the situation, emotionally scarred. Brian's anguish was something I had no difficulty in understanding. Many of the lurid images from the time my own father was in the doldrums seemed to superimpose themselves on what was happening to my family.

I can not put into words the sheer, deep-rooted misery of that period and the trauma I personally underwent in my desperate bid to literally keep the roof over our heads. And it was raining, not cats and dogs but bankers and lawyers. I could now understand better the pain and frustration that my own father went through when I was young. It felt as if history was about to repeat itself and teach me a lesson on life.

With the dawning of each dismal day I struggled against the legal onslaught of those who think nothing of kicking you, and bloody hard, when you are down. The pressure was enormous. I felt that I was a failure and it was beginning to affect me. I developed serious chest pains and, fearing the worst, I ended up spending a few weeks in hospital. Luckily this was diagnosed as a panic attack and I was given a clean bill of health. However, at 29, it felt

Val Deane, who changed my life, walking in Scotland.

as if my world was falling apart and at an end.

Sitting in my office one morning, sifting through the day's mail, most of which provided little or no solace, I was gratefully distracted, albeit briefly, by the arrival of Val Deane, the father of a secretary working for me at the time, Valerie. He just dropped by for a casual chat but I suspect, as I look back, that maybe Valerie had told him of my deepening despair and depression and this was his attempt to cheer me up.

Val, a widower, is one of the most gregarious people I have ever met. He has a *bonhomie* which is especially typical of the people living on Cork city's north side where families still opt to live in close clusters, where the sense of community is sacrosanct and where humour permeates every situation. He is also the type of man of whom it could be said, without malice, that he would 'talk the cross off a donkey'.

On this particular day, Val was doing all the talking while I sat there feigning interest, with my mind focused on the grim affairs of the recent past. I was depressed and frustrated with a deeply-rooted sense of failure. This awful feeling, which welled-up inside me, seemed to consume any resolve I had left.

'Pat, you should really get away from the office once in a while. Get out more, become involved in something other than the business ...' Val went on. 'Have you ever been hill walking? Now, there's something you should try. What about next Sunday? I'm going walking then, why don't you come along?'

I seemed to recall, at that moment, Valerie telling me sometime previously about her dad being part of a local group called Cork Mountaineering, but their activities were something I never gave a second thought to. My sole interests had, for some considerable time, been work and money. Recreation and hobbies provided no financial reward so I never saw the point in pursuing these.

As Val kept up his banter and repeated his invitation, I turned to him, in my trance-like state. 'Yeah. I'll go,' I replied with all the sincerity I could cobble together in my attempt to, well, to be honest, just get him to go away and leave me alone.

'Great stuff! I'll give you a call on Friday just to confirm the details,' and off he went.

Friday came and so did Val's telephone call. 'How are you Pat?' he inquired, not waiting for an answer. 'We're all meeting outside the Opera House at half past eight on Sunday morning. All you need to bring are boots, rain gear, sandwiches and yourself. I'll see you there.' And with that he hung up.

Well fuck me! I thought, what have I got myself into?

I drove to the rendezvous that bright Sunday morning feeling neither disinclined nor eager. I had given my word and I was going to stick by it.

Outside the Opera House I met Val and his walking buddies who did not at all tally with my preconceived notion of what mountaineers should look like. Here was a diverse age group from all walks of life. My distinct and initial feeling was that I had nothing in common with these people. At the time the word 'yuppie' had not yet been coined but that's what I felt like – a 'yuppie' among a coterie whose interests transcended those of the commercial world.

Introductions were made and the group chatted in what I thought was an idle manner of past walks and future hiking plans. Eventually, a small convoy of cars headed west for Kerry. As we crossed the county boundary one of my passengers remarked on the clear skies and how inviting the hills looked. And, for the first time ever, despite having travelled this road many times before, I consciously noticed the splendour of the hills which straddle the border between Cork and Kerry.

'Those are The Paps, Pat.' I could see where the name came from as the two hills rose like two gigantic breasts out of the barren landscape.

Later, I discovered that the association of this geographical feature with certain parts of the female anatomy was as old as time. In pre-Christian Ireland these hills were known as *Da Chioch*

Dhana, meaning the 'Two Breasts of Dana', and she was the mother of the ancient gods.

Half an hour later Val directed me up a series of winding bohereens to a clearance near a remote sheep farmer's cottage.

'Here we are Pat. This is the starting point of the walk. It's not a particularly long one, it should only take about four to five hours depending on how many sandwiches you'll have to stop and eat,' he quipped.

The thought of walking across sheep-studded mountain bog for five hours did not exactly apply heat to the cockles of my heart as we left the car to join the others in the party. But, as we gradually headed up the hillside towards Gleann na gCapall, The Horses' Glen, I began to register sounds, sights and even smells which, for reasons I could not then rationalise, were as new and wondrous to me as the first sensory experiences of a baby coming into the world.

The light early morning breeze carried the pungent odours of the nearby farmyard mixed with the scent of the pine trees that had been planted as a shelter belt around the nearby farmhouse. I listened to the sound of birdsong and the gentle fall of cascading water from the hills as it made its way to the sea. The bright yellow flowers of the gorse which grew at the foot of the hills and the scattered mats of purple heather which had somehow escaped the voracious grazing of the mountain sheep, contrasted sharply against the brown mountain bog. These are among my memories of that first day on the hills.

The further we walked, the more dispersed the group became and I found myself alone for much of the trek taking in the views which began to dramatically uncloak with every hundred feet or so we climbed. We headed up the ridge towards Stoompa, a double-headed hill which at its highest point is some 695 metres (2,281 feet) above sea level. Behind me the spell-weaving beauty of Muckross Lake and Lough Guitane and below, deep in the glen, the necklace formation of Lough Garagarry, Lough Managh and Lough Erhogh drained all negative thoughts from my mind.

For the first time in a long period I felt cheerful. I was at peace with myself and felt in harmony with these tranquil surroundings. My exhilaration increased as we scrambled up a rock strewn incline towards the boggy plateau from which Mangerton rose at 840 metres (2,756 feet), the highest point on the walk.

The walkers stopped here to enjoy flasks of hot tea and sandwiches on the remote, barren and weathered hilltop. The conversation touched on diverse subjects but none of a serious nature. The mood was decidedly jovial. Somebody remarked that in earlier generations when people lost their way on the hills they turned their coats inside out believing this would act as a charm setting them in the right direction.

'But what if you were wearing a reversible jacket. Would you end up going round in circles?' I joked.

Standing atop Mangerton I was elated – I had succeeded in climbing my first mountain. For the first time in months, I had set my sights on a goal and had achieved my objective and I was proud of this.

The views on all sides were breathtaking. But my attention was particularly drawn to a cluster of mountains to the west of us.

'What are they called, Val?'

'Those are the Macgillycuddy's Reeks and the biggest one is Corrán Tuathail, which, at 1,039 metres (3,414 feet), is Ireland's highest peak. I suppose you'll want to walk up that one next.'

'Do you think I could?'

'Not today,' he replied with a smile. 'But maybe next weekend.'

From that moment on all my thoughts focused on Corrán Tuathail and what was for me at that time an impending adventure of great magnitude. My next goal was to reach its summit. This task gave me a sense of purpose and direction.

The following week was unbearably long. I lay awake each night with all the restless excitement of a child on Christmas Eve, wondering what treasures will be under the tree the next morning. I was also slightly fearful of what lay ahead. I could not wait to get back on the hills and more especially to climb the highest mountain in Ireland. This was to be my Everest.

I rang Val a couple of times that week to confirm that the walk was on for the following Sunday, realising the irony of the sudden reversal of roles. Firing off a barrage of questions on what lay ahead, I started to focus on the potential problems I could encounter on my trek to the top of Ireland.

Stimulated by the idea of climbing Corrán Tuathail, I was also uneasy about the fact that I had walked away from my problems without ever having solved them. Subconsciously I knew this was the right thing to do. I had to take time out, to clear my head and re-organise my mental energies. I needed, badly, to taste success. The planning and preparation was in place and I knew I could do it – climb to the top. The week speedily rolled by and, at last, the morning of our climb dawned.

I threw my climbing boots and rain gear into the boot of my car and headed west where, upon seeing the 'Welcome To Kerry' road sign at the county boundary, my spirits rose towards the tops of the mountains for which I was starting to develop a consuming passion.

The border between Counties Cork and Kerry would become an important psychological stepping stone over the next number of years. Once I crossed this line my mind would become untroubled and relaxed and I would rekindle an ability to solve problems. Walking and climbing in a totally uncluttered and natural environment enhanced my ability to function efficiently as a businessman once again.

THE MOUNTAIN MAN

When I behold your mountains bold –
Your noble lakes and streams –
A mingled tide of grief and pride
Within my bosom teems.

O'Hagan

The sheep jokes had stopped about twenty minutes earlier. We now struggled silently against driving winds and the thick mists which swirled above our heads. We picked our way precariously up a steep scree-covered slope cut by gullies sculpted by aeons of wet days just like this. I had not yet got my 'second wind' and as we trudged onwards and upwards, my lungs burned with each heaving breath. Perspiration ran down my face, chest and back and I began to wonder why I was wearing a rain-proof jacket and leggings when I felt as wet inside my clothes as outside.

We made good time as far as the first hill top, Cnoc an Bhráca, 731 metres (2,398 feet), but now on the approach to Cruach Mhór, 932 metres (3,062 feet), I marvelled not so much at the rugged mountain landscape as at the agile and unfaltering progress being made by my guide and companion, Val Deane.

The slope ended at Cruach Mhór where I was surprised to see a Marian Grotto. I would encounter similar expressions of devotion years later during my expeditions in the Himalaya. There the deities had exotic names but the sentiment of the faithful was the same as though Tom Sullivan who had trudged up this steep slope with the materials to construct this shrine.

I stood there, my lungs heaving to catch my breath, questioning the wisdom of tackling Ireland's highest mountain, Corrán Tuathail, so soon after my introduction to hill walking. The smokey-grey blanket of mist dissipated into the valley below and with the suddenness of a projector flashing a celluloid image onto a cinema screen, a rugged and seemingly ethereal mountain landscape revealed itself. This was definitely more mountain than hill – an imposing backbone of 350 million year-old red sandstone out of which time and the elements had carved pinnacles, clefts, gullies, towers, cirques and erratic rock shapes to trigger the imagination.

'We're almost at the most exciting stage, Pat,' said Val, as we made our approach onto the first of two knife-edged arêtes broken by the 988 metres (3,191 feet) peak of Cnoc na Peiste, Hill of the Serpent. Far below us the light caught the metal grey surface of the corrie lake known as Coimin na Peiste, also named after the same folkloric beast from which this ridge took its name.

I had never before experienced such exhilaration as I hiked along the high ridge which snaked towards our eventual goal. The trauma of losing my business and having the hurtful task of laying off my workers was not erased from my mind but I began to finally realise that life, like the very mountains I walked on, was a series of highs and lows, ups and downs. The physical effort of walking these hills and the scrambling over precipitous rock was beginning to create a feeling of well-being in my body and soul. Away from the office and pressures of home, I found I could bring about a mental equilibrium, an ability to separate the wheat from the chaff of my thoughts.

Now that most of the hard work was behind us, Val and I laughed and joked as the ridge widened and we followed the edges of a series of north-facing coombes. These funnelled the accumulated rainwater from the tops of the mountains into Lough Cailee, the Hag's Lake, at the head of the Hag's Glen.

'A tourist was being taken on a tour of the 'Reeks by a local man. Heading up the Hag's Glen the guide pointed to a hill and said: "that there is Corrán Tuathail, the highest mountain in Ireland." The tourist looked at the hill and noticed, nearby, another which was obviously much higher. "I think you must be mistaken, Sir. That one over there looks tallest," said the disbelieving tourist. "I know it does, but Corrán Tuathail is standing in a hollow," said the guide.' I waited for Val's reaction to the only joke I knew about these mountains.

'And I was beginning to believe you hadn't one clean joke,' was his riposte.

'Below us there is the Devil's Ladder,' Val said, bringing my attention to one of the most popular access and exit points on the mountain, 'and just above us is the top, the place where the sky begins.'

We walked across a boggy saddle and before us rose the great barren head of Corrán Tuathail. The last stage was nothing demanding or, maybe I was so overcome with excitement that I never felt its physical impact. Before long, Val was shaking my hand and complimenting me on my achievement as we stood under the huge metal cross which marks Ireland's highest ground. I clenched my fists and punched the air with a shout of proud achievement – 'yes, I've done it!'

Taking in the views which formed the rich tapestry of land, lakes, rivers and sea I turned to my companion and said, 'Val, I am going to climb Everest one of these days.'

He looked at me and smiled and said nothing, knowing that many people go to the mountains to dream. But this for me was no delusion. There and then I had made my mind up as my grandmother's wise words came into my head – 'if you think you can, you will. If you think you can't, you won't.'

I would return to the top of Corrán Tuathail many more times in the coming years, enjoying its peace and tranquillity in the company of people with whom I have been privileged to cross mountain paths. But that first day on the mountain with Val Deane is one I will always remember with special fondness. This was an important turning point in my life. It was also the day I learned a valuable lesson – that you can never appreciate what it is like to stand on the highest mountain until you have been in the deepest valley.

From that moment on I became more and more immersed in a world which previously I never knew existed. Sometimes I went on casual, easy going hill walks, other times I embarked on extreme climbs, becoming more and more adventurous, pushing myself to the very limit of my endurance. New acquaintances entered my life, people from varied backgrounds and of many nationalities with whom I shared my passion for the highlands. And, my fondness for the Kerry 'Reeks eventually led to the forging of lasting and treasured friendships with those who live in the shelter of those hills.

Towards the close of my first year hill walking and climbing, this activity had become my passion and therapy, the panacea to all my ills. This was not escapism. If I had a problem to solve or a decision to make, I took it to the mountain and returned, invariably, with the best decision or solution I could reach.

I enrolled in a mountain leadership course eager to learn all the skills necessary for navigation and survival in all conditions. The syllabus included a field trip with the voluntary Kerry Mountain Rescue team during which I first encountered a man who was to become my mentor and close friend.

When I next encountered Con Moriarty he was standing behind the counter of his shop in Killarney, a huge, hairy, hulking figure with a charm and smile which could melt a hole through the most ancient permafrost. At the time he was selling climbing equipment, boots and all-weather gear from his 'Mountain Man' shop in Killarney. He was also on the brink of launching his 'Hidden Ireland' tour company, offering guided walks through some of the most historic and environmentally unique and remote parts of western Ireland. It was not difficult to grasp how he had earned the moniker 'mountain man'. Standing at six feet five inches, in his washed feet, with long hair and full beard I thought him the embodiment of those legendary pre-Christian tribesmen who placed massive stone upon stone in the construction of imposing Celtic monuments like the fort of Dun Aonghus on the Aran Islands.

We chatted amicably about the hills with that distinct though genial wariness which Kerry people display towards Corkonians, and vice versa, on their first encounter. In the course of our conversation it was obvious that there existed between us a unique empathy. So much so in fact that there and then he suggested we take to the hills. In a series of impulsive gestures he grabbed his rucksack and jacket and ushered me out onto the footpath, making sure to hang his 'Sorry, Closed To Go Climbing' sign on the door.

Swept along on Con's wave of enthusiasm I found myself, that same day, scrambling up Collins' Gully, a water-worn wrinkle in the rock on the north-eastern face of Corrán Tuathail, a route which provided a steep and exciting stairway to the summit. Later, as we headed back through the Hag's Glen and along the banks of the Gaddagh River, Con and I agreed to meet the following weekend and do some 'serious climbing'.

Born in the Gap of Dunloe, one of the most tranquil and ruggedly beautiful places on earth, Con had an atavistic 'feel' for the mountains coupled with a deep knowledge of their people, history and folklore. But his interests transcended the country of his birth to the far flung mountain regions of South America, Central Europe and Asia.

Invariably, we would finish many of our rock climbing and hill walking outings discussing, over pints of black stout in some Kerry pub, the exploits of the great climbers of the past like Tenzing, Hunt, Lowe, Shipton, Messner and, of course, the epoch-making New Zealand beekeeper, Edmund Hillary. We spoke in admiration of Reinhold Messner and Peter Habeler who in May, 1978 climbed Everest without oxygen, and other devoted mountaineers who provided further fuel to feed our fires of ambition.

By now, I was a voluntary member of Kerry Mountain Rescue and was beginning to acquire the skills needed for more and more adventurous undertakings in high places. Proficiency at climbing can only

Con Moriarty, whose infectious love of mountains and their people inspired me, on expedition in Irian Jaya.

be achieved through long, hard hours of practice exposed to all-weather conditions and pitted against all types of mountainous terrain. The tragic fatalities I encountered while working with the search were a grim illustration of the things that could go horribly wrong due to ill judgement, faulty equipment or, most often, lack of experience.

On one occasion, during a search at the base of high cliffs to the east of Corrán Tuathail, Con, Mary MacGillycuddy – a member of Kerry Mountain Rescue from Killorglin – and I made the gruesome discovery of the body of a British hill walker who had been reported missing almost six months previously. The lone walker had chosen the Devil's Ladder as his route to the top. We assumed, judging from the place where the remains were found, that he had made it to the highest point of his walk but, on the descent, had lost his way and dropped from the edge of the precipitous cliff. The corpse was in a state of advanced decomposition. We placed the remains in a body bag and carried it to a waiting hearse at

Lislebane.

Gradually, I came to understand that in order to survive on the mountains, certain, fundamental skills were needed. Jumping at every opportunty to take to the mountains with experienced climbers and walkers, I quickly acquired mountain craft. The first lesson I learned was that those who go to the mountains must take responsibility for their own well-being and safety – don't walk into a potentially dangerous situation unless you have the proficiency to get yourself back out again, was the golden rule.

In the company of Con and other experienced mountaineers I learned the techniques necessary for rock and ice climbing and night and zero visibility navigation with map and compass. I conditioned myself to less romantic moments like sleeping in damp caves, manure covered barns or, simply stuffed in a plastic refuse sack under the stars.

Having powerful waves breaking against your backside as you dangle from the end of a rope fixed to a sea cliff might not seem the most comforting of experiences. But with Con shouting curse-laden encouragement from the top, I found that even this can have a certain element of fun. People do not climb merely to endure and overcome extreme physical and mental obstacles. One main driving force is the satisfaction and pleasure which can be derived when the challenge to overcome the worst is vanquished.

'Falvey, will you get your ass out of the water and up here. What are you trying to do, catch mackerel?'

As I unclipped from my belay point on the rock face I could hear Con roaring with laughter from his considerably drier and higher position on the cliff face. He was watching a huge wave heading for the headland on which we clung. It was obvious to him that this mass of angry water would break against my backside. Just then the big breaker hit me with enough force to send me shooting fifteen feet up the rock wall. On that occasion I can remember being very relieved to make it, as quickly as possible, to the top where our laughter completely erased the near panic I had felt earlier.

Another memory always brings a smile to my face. It happened in the Rabach's Glen near the Healy Pass in County Cork's remote Beara Peninsula. This area takes its name from Sean an Rabach, which roughly translated means Sean the Savage, who was said to be the last man hung in the province of Munster for murder.

We had run a 1,000-feet long cable from a crag, which hung about 500 feet above the ground, across very rough terrain to a clear position at the bottom. We intended to practice getting a seriously-injured person off the mountain as quickly and as gently as possible. One volunteer descended the acutely-angled cable, or rope, in a stretcher making it to the ground anchor point without a hitch. The remainder of us on the crag were to harness ourselves to the rope and follow suit, one at a time. I was the third, and I think the heaviest, to go. Everything went smoothly until I slid downwards along the section of the cable which shot over the ruined stone house of the Rabach.

Kerry Mountain Rescue, who gave me essential training and experience, in action.

I was coming in at speed and those on the other end of the brake rope, attached to my waist, had jokingly paid out too much slack. I suddenly realised I was on a collision course with the gable end of the ruin. I raised my legs, akimbo, to act as a bumper. Adding to my distress was the fact that about sixty people had entered the glen and were now standing around the Rabach's house watching my Harold Lloyd-like flight through the air. Sure enough, because my G-force produced sag in the rope, I hit the top of the gable sending cut stones crashing to the ground below. Amazingly, I arrived at the cable's end suffering no more than acute embarrassment. This became even more intense when I discovered the by-standers were not there to observe a search and rescue team but were part of a guided tour of places of historic interest, one of which I had just partially demolished. On that occasion, I applied my skills as a stone mason to obvious advantage, restoring the damaged wall on the landmark cottage and saving a little face in the process.

The seven years I spent with Kerry Mountain Rescue were times I will always treasure. I made many friends, people with a similar outlook who shared my passion for adventure, travel and climbing. 'You cannot be a good mountaineer, however great your ability, unless you are cheerful and have the spirit of comradeship. Friends are as important as achievement,' Tenzing once said. I find these words of wisdom ring true, especially in my experiences with my friends in Kerry.

My climbing successes enabled me to look at my business in a more relaxed manner and formulate a course of action which would enable me to solve my deep-rooted financial problems. The greatest obstacle I had to overcome was the admission that I was flat broke. It was not easy to accept that everything was gone but once I faced up to the reality of the situation, I had a solid foundation on which to reconstruct my life. Mine was not abject failure. I had made many mistakes but with each one I had learned something and upon my re-entry to the business world would not be victim to the same snares.

If you fail to summit a mountain all you can do is try another time. You cannot, on your second or subsequent attempts, start from your previous highest elevation – you have to commence from the bottom. In business the same applies and I discovered that the immediate solution to my dilemma was to begin where I began in the first place – on 'the line', working as a block layer.

On a basic level this enabled me to provide for my family. I gave up all the ostentatious trappings of the showy businessman. No more wine-washed business luncheons with self-obsessed financiers and lawyers. I now ate my sandwiches with the lads on 'the line'.

The threat of losing my house hung over my head on a tenuous thread. For the next few years I worked like an automaton to earn enough money to keep the baying bankers at bay. Most Friday evenings I would throw my boots, tent, sleeping bag and rain gear into the back of the car and head off for the mountains, returning by 8am the following Monday morning rejuvenated and ready to restore my success as a businessman – block by block.

RESCUED IN THE ALPS

For the genuine mountaineer, whether he be stuck like a fly on a wall in the most desperate of situations or regarding the view on an easy stroll, making a first ascent or the hundred and first, it is enough that he is there.

Ronald Clark

'Oh Jesus! Falvey don't fall. Please don't fall. You'll kill both of us.'

I could clearly hear Con Moriarty's expletive-peppered prayer as I was about to swing, a human pendulum, across the face of the ice wall. It was dark. I was exhausted and had never been more terrified in my life as I was negotiating the frozen cliff face. Edging towards my partner, my darkest fear was realised. I fell, head first, fifty feet into a black abyss having lost my footing while trying to traverse to where Con was on an airy belay cut from the ice. I hung there wondering how much longer my big Kerry friend could hold on from his precarious perch higher up. Here I was, on my first expedition to the Alps, wondering if this would also be my last.

Along with Ivan Counihan, a young climber from Kerry and Tim Flavin, an experienced sea kayak sailor, Con and I decided, in 1989, to stage a winter holiday training and perfecting our ice-climbing skills on the Alps and do a few mountain routes. One of these was on the north face of the Aiguille du Midi, which lies to the east of Mont Blanc. We knew this was regarded as a classic route but, here, my knowledge of this Alpine mass more or less began and ended.

I arrived in Chamonix, France relatively unprepared with all the undisciplined enthusiasm of a school child on a field trip. Once our gear and ourselves were checked in at the cheapest lodgings we could find, one of the boys jokingly declared, 'right lads, let's go on the *piste*'.

In the ten days we spent in and around Chamonix, I got no more than twenty hours sleep such was the punishing schedule of ice climbing and carousing we set for ourselves. At the time I thought little of the impression we, a raggle taggle group of Irishmen, must have made as we mingled with the clearly affluent and distinctly colour co-ordinated skiers and climbers with whom we shared various modes of public transport.

However, there was one occasion when I felt a little self-conscious, if not distinctly mortified. The previous evening we had over-indulged in one of the many fine hostelries in Chamonix. And, hungover and dehydrated from potent Swiss beer, here we were, the day after the night before, about to catch a cable car to take us to the starting point of a route in the Glacier d'Argentiere when Moriarty began unmercifully slagging Counihan. Con felt his colleague was dragging behind or, dragging his behind. I cannot remember exactly which but on this particular morning the big fellah was giving Ivan a relentless haranguing. 'Will you hurry on, we're going to miss the cable car at this rate,' he bellowed. To this Ivan, suffering from a hangover, would only reply – 'ah! fuck off!'

The cable car was almost full when we finally raced to its doors, unceremoniously jumped in and, encumbered with overflowing rucksacks and coils of rope, collided with most of the other forty passengers.

'We nearly missed it. What did I tell you?'

At this stage, Ivan, who is some inches shorter than Moriarty, could take no more. With every comment made by his aggressor he jumped into the air to bark, nose to nose with Moriarty and repeated his earlier riposte.

The car swung with every jump. The silent, well-groomed passengers, who clearly were not suffering the negative after-effects of alcohol, looked on in bemused wonder and maybe even a little trepidation as the two lads snarled at each other like a terrier and a bear in a pit. We disembarked, much to the relief of our fellow passengers I'm sure, but the two lads kept it up, even when roped together.

Two days later, we returned to our digs with the intention of taking on, the following morning, the Mallory route on the Midi – an exciting and demanding route. After a fairly punishing few days on the slopes it would have been prudent for us to retire early and get a good night's rest before the climb. But, after a shower, a change of clothes and a square meal we – apart from Flavin who had more sense than the rest of us put together – got into an intriguing conversation until the wee hours with a bunch of Polish climbers. At 6am, after about three hours sleep, Flavin woke us for breakfast and was met with a flood of groans, grunts and collective malediction against his cheerfulness. An alcohol-induced fug filled my head as I struggled to get my gear ready for the high point of our whole trip. Ivan decided to stay in Chamonix and do some skiing instead.

We caught the cable car to Plan De'Laguille and were climbing by 9am. After the first couple of hundred feet, I felt none of the physical repercussions of our night on the tiles. With each hour picking our way through the fresh snow, roped together like a string of pack mules, the gradient became steeper and steeper but our impression, as far as gaining height was concerned, seemed to be minimal.

Darkness had fallen and with it the air temperature but we continued. By 10pm hunger and exhaustion forced me into a torpor. I acted like an automaton, plunging with clock-work repetition the handle of my ice axe into the névé before each step and maintaining my equidistance between Con and Tim. With each footfall of my cramponed boot I exhaled a clearly visible puff of hot, moist breath which blew back into my face turning to frost on my eyebrows, beard and on the tip of my nose. The climbing had been interesting but the day very long. After a brief 11pm respite, sitting in the snow drinking liquids to counteract our dehydration after thirteen hours on the go, we were back on our feet.

'That's it – I'm off the drink. Never again. I'm taking the pledge once we get back home,' Con declared, not for the first time. He then led off on the next section of the climb until all of the fifty metre rope was paid out. Using an ice screw to fasten his rope to the almost sheer icy face of the mountain, he called – 'right Falvey, climb when ready.'

I heard him faintly in the distant darkness. Unable to see him and barely able to catch his voice, I bade my farewell to Tim and followed the rope which disappeared into the black night directly above my head. I used my ice axe and the fanged tip of my crampons with an intensity prompted by my survival instinct. Moving cautiously, I scrambled upwards to where the rope was attached to an ice screw. At that point I came to an abrupt halt at the base of a black cliff and I wondered where Moriarty was on that huge canvas of cold rock.

A pin-prick of light from Con's head torch weakly pierced the darkness and revealed his position. I estimated his distance to be about fifty feet directly to my right. I removed the ice screw and, crab like, started my traverse towards the dot of light. Everything had gone like clockwork and I was feeling elated on this climb through the star-studded night. The axe, which I held in my right hand buried itself in the ice. Then, as I took a step with my right foot, kicking the spiked toe into the almost impenetrable black ice, the bale which fastened one crampon to my boot broke away. 'Shit! I'm in trouble now,' I thought to myself.

'Con, be ready to hold a fall,' I shouted, never really expecting such an eventuality. 'I've just lost a bale.' The remainder of the crampon hung loosely from the heel of my boot, useless.

'You can't fall. Hold on, for Christ's sake, I'm only held to the ice by two screws and I don't know if they'll hold,' he angrily responded, mindful of the fact that Tim was roped on behind me.

A fall at this potentially perilous juncture would have taken all three of us down the steep face and Tim had no idea what was happening to me high above him on the ice. If I took a dive, taking Moriarty with me, there was no way Tim could resist the terrifying tug he would consequently receive on his end of the rope.

'Bunny-hop Falvey. Bunny-hop.' Trying to regain my balance, I placed my right foot on top of my left, which still had a hold on the ice, and attempted to swing both legs as one while hanging on to the ice axes. My left foot failed to gain purchase. The force of my two-legged kick dislodged the axe I held in my right hand. I spun out of control and dangled precariously 2,000 feet high on the face.

How long could I hold on like this? I knew the answer as soon as I had asked myself the question. My life did not flash before my eyes in that instant but I firmly believed this was it, the end, the fat lady had just sung her song.

'Jesus Christ! Con, I'm going to fall,' I screamed, afraid that the power of my voice colliding on the icy, lifeless rock just inches from my face would jemmy me from my perilous and single connection with the mountain. I instantly swung my axe in a desperate bid to regain my balance.

'Falvey don't fall. Please, please Falvey, don't fucking fall – you'll kill all of us,' he shouted back, informing me in clipped, brief terms that he was standing on a tiny groove, which he had cut into the ice slope and was secured by just two ice screws. And then, my blood ran cold when I realised his position was far from secure. As I struggled to pull myself back into a slightly stronger situation I shouted a warning to Con – 'be prepared for a hard tug' – and I silently prayed that he would somehow be able to hold me.

'Falvey, swing your ice axe and get a hold.' There was little else I could do.

The metal pick of the axe failed to bury itself into the hard ice. The force of the hammer-like action dislodged my other axe and I shot down the side of the mountain, head first, thinking to meet my fate. With no time to consider the full and potentially fatal implications of my predicament, I savagely jerked to a halt with a snap of the rope. Like a bungee-jumper I sprung, upside down, on the end of my life-line, which miraculously held.

The hairs on the back of my neck stiffened with terror like the spikes on a hedgehog as the blood rushed to my head and my racing pulse beat out a rhythm of panic in my eardrums. Looking down at the lights of Chamonix far below, I swung like a plumb-line in a storm. After what seemed like an interminable period but was in reality mere seconds, a rush of adrenalin flushed through my body. I pushed with both feet against the ice wall at my back and, like a circus performer on the high wire, did an aerobatic flip to bring myself upright. With all the strength I could muster, I slammed my axes into the ice face in what I knew would be my only hope to relieve the pressure on the rope now being anchored by Moriarty. I desperately clawed myself upwards.

'Falvey. Falvey, are you allright?' came the voice from on high.

In shock and unable to determine my next move, I helplessly pleaded with him – 'keep a tight rope.'

Slowly, I began the difficult task of climbing with just one crampon towards his eyrie. By the time I made it to Con's perch, I was emotionally and physically drained. I felt as if someone had unscrewed my toes and all my energy, spirit and confidence had just, somehow, drained from my body.

'I knew you could do it, Falvey boy,' came Con's words of reassurance.

But, I could not go on, I had to recover. I found it unbearably hard to perform a simple task like clipping myself to Con's belay point. My entire body shook like a jack-hammer and my muscles turned to jelly.

'Make sure I've clipped in correctly.' Con checked the steel crab joining my harness to the belay stance and fixed me securely as he belayed Tim to our position. Once that was done, we decided to find a ledge and stop for the night, having had quite enough drama for one day and badly needing some well-earned rest.

We continued to work our way horizontally across the ice when misfortune reared its ugly head yet again.

'Dear Jesus, this can't be happening,' I uttered as, well into this traverse, my harness slipped down around my ankles. I tried to pull it back into position with one hand while holding onto a lip of rock with my other. Hobbled on the rock outcrop I felt like thirteen stone of dead weight, an impediment adding to the already extreme workload of my colleagues. The sheer force of my sudden weight on the harness buckle, when I hung upside down, had somehow caused the strap to run through just enough to work loose, despite the fact that it had been doubled back.

Imagine you are having a bowel movement in the woods when suddenly a huge, angry bear comes crashing through the undergrowth. You feebly run for dear life with your trousers down around your ankles. Well, that was how I felt, sort of. In my particular predicament there was no bear but the dread in my heart was fed by the huge drop just below me. Holding on with one hand on the rock, I bent down to pull up the harness but with each sideward step the damn thing would fall down again.

'Con, this is hopeless. I can't go any further,' I said with bitter resignation.

Trying to remove the harness, I was prevented by the spikes on my only remaining crampon which seemed to bite into the leg loops like a dog with a bone. Moriarty tied-off his belay, came alongside me and helped me to secure the harness around my waist. We scrambled along the exposed rock outcrop in search of a ledge on which to spend the remainder of the night. High above Chamonix we 'bivvied', tied to a vertical rock face and as exposed as limpets on a sea boulder at low tide. While bedding down, Flavin's lightweight and flimsy plastic 'bivvy' bag split up the middle. My last sight, before closing my eyes for a few hours sleep, was of him emptying his rucksack which he then pulled down over his head and shoulders, having already wrapped his legs and feet in the torn 'bivvy' bag. What great fellows to be on the mountains with, I thought and I slept fitfully and briefly.

Three hours later we were readying ourselves for the final leg of the assault. Con had awoken to the agonising pain of frost-nipped toes and we all agreed to get to the top as quickly and safely as possible and back to Chamonix.

As we progressed up the mounain, the malicious spectre of bad luck stayed with me. My second crampon broke and fell away as we were about to negotiate a large, steeply-inclined ice field. At this stage, Tim had only one crampon, I had none and the odds were unfairly stacked against us on our ice climb. The particular brand of crampon we used on that occasion was later withdrawn from the market when, following complaints I lodged with the British Mountaineering Council, an investigation was set in motion which found a serious design fault in the product.

There was another option which we briefly discussed – avoid the ice field by climbing the vertical rock band which stopped just shy of the top. With little rock climbing gear in our possession we nonetheless felt this was our best alternative.

Like flies on a wall, we made it to within 120 feet of the cable car station atop the Midi but were stopped dead in our vertical tracks by an overhang of rock which, without the proper equipment, we could not negotiate. There was no going back, of that we were certain – not with a cable car within reach, if we just had a rope. So, as we loitered on the rock outcrop, Con in his best Kerry accent and broken French, bellowed to the top for some kind soul to throw down a line.

The cable car attendant heard our cries but was ignorant of the Gap of Dunloe French dialect and did not understand our request. He shouted something down to us but similarly none of us could understand what he had said. 'Well, at least they know we are here,' I uttered.

We waited and waited, with no choice to do otherwise, hoping to see the welcoming end of a rope come dangling down from the enormous brow of rock on the face of the mountain. But nothing happened. Then, as we waited bored stiff and in a state of exposed desperation, the air shook with a thunderous, thumping vibration as above our heads a helicopter hovered into view. The cable car attendant, misinterpreting our cries, had alerted the mountain rescue service thinking we were in imminent danger.

There are many people, like some of those who operate *le tele-cabine*, who cannot comprehend why somebody would choose to climb a mountain and expose themselves to a certain degree of risk when perfectly good modes of mechanical transport have been provided to carry them to the summit.

The chopper could not get a line to us directly, because of the overhead cables, so a member of the crew was dropped on the summit and, with officious French efficiency he oversaw us as we were winched to the top, providing an added attraction for the hundreds of day trippers on the Midi.

Safe at last, my first reaction, after all we had been through, was to call home. I was glad we had made it but, I was now anxious to get back to work. Lessons well learned will never be forgotten. We bid farewell to Chamonix. Our experience had provided newly-acquired knowledge which we would take with us on future expeditions. The drama provided by this adventure was an integral part of any climber's apprenticeship. Accidents could be caused by a myriad of factors. We began to realise, forcefully, that the primary objective in mountaineering was not only to reach the top but return safely to the bottom.

Marie told me on the telephone that she had received an urgent message for Con to contact his family and once I had given her a potted account of our adventure, omitting detail about the close encounters with disaster, we said our goodbyes.

When Moriarty walked out of the cable car terminal towards us minutes later it was obvious from the expression on his face that something was terribly wrong. He had just been told the tragic news of a fellow climber's death in Ireland. Adrian Devlin, a newly married close friend, had been killed in a road traffic accident while returning from an adventure in the Burren, County Clare. We were all devastated by the news, but none more so than Con. I could not help but consider the odd perplexity of life at that moment. We had just played a game of cat and mouse with death and came out winners, while a close friend, in a cruel twist of fate, never made it home from his trip to the west of Ireland.

THE EIGER

Though much is taken, much abides
And though we are not now that strength which in olden
days moved Earth
and Heaven,
That which we are, we are
One equal temper of heroic hearts
Made weak by time and fate,
But strong in will
To strive, to seek, to find, and not to yield.

Alfred, Lord Tennyson

I honed my snow and ice climbing skills anywhere I could find a suitable challenge and Himalayan-like conditions within relatively easy reach. Most of these sorties were to Scotland during the winter months. However, a chance meeting in Cork with a leading professional climber from Wales, Pat Littlejohn, led to an attempt on the Eiger in January, 1991. Our plan, which included the well-known Irish mountaineer Eddie Cooper from Belfast, was to climb the Lauper Route on the north face of this mountain. This, I decided, would be a crucial evaluation of my climbing ability prior to the Ama Dablam expedition.

The mountain we chose has inspired not only climbers but writers, painters and Hollywood film makers like Clint Eastwood. In 1975, Eastwood directed himself in the role of an art lecturer cum assassin hired to carry out a contract on its thickly verglassed rock in a movie called *The Eiger Sanction.*

We arrived in Switzerland having spent time at an international gathering of ice climbers in the Vallon di Cogne, one of Northern Italy's most popular training grounds.

Our first view of the cold north face was disheartening. These Alpine giants are not always white. Sometimes they are black and to our intense aggravation the Lauper route was totally shrouded in a dark cloak of ice, a chilling divination of the fatal consequences which would certainly result from a climb on ice like this.

'It's too dangerous. Why don't we give Clint Eastwood a call

and see what he thinks?' I said to Littlejohn, attempting to resuscitate our battered morale.

As the more experienced climber he had veto over our plan.
His decision, which I fully supported, was to kibosh Plan A.

'Sorry guys, but I've been here before and if conditions on the
north face are not spot on you're wasting your time in any attempt
to climb it.'

Of course, I was disappointed to hear this but mountains, like
lots of things in life, have more than one face. There are few mountaineers I know of who will not quickly dispel any disappointment
felt when a plan does not come together due to forces, like climat-
ic conditions, which are outside their control. Without the support
of Mother Nature no climb can succeed no matter how well
equipped and skilled the expedition members are. And, to disregard the weather conditions is to court disaster. So, following the
advice of some old sage we let Nature be our teacher and immediately set about putting an alternative Eiger plan together.

Any agitation I may have felt at being denied the opportunity
to assault the north face was dissolved in the growing enthusiasm
for Plan B – the south ridge. Our research did not show this route
to be in any way an inferior challenge. On the contrary, the guide
books were unanimous in describing the sections between the two
Eigerjock saddles, as the stuff of minor epics in winter conditions.
In fact, many teams had called it a day having failed to cross this
knife-edge ridge, especially in winter conditions.

Our day on the mountain was delayed by 24 hours when,
despite perfect weather, we missed the train from Grindelwald to
Kleiner Scheidegg, the last outpost before the great mountain.
Having found that the earliest train the following day would leave
from Lauterbrunnen we decided to spend the night there.

Sitting in a café that same evening we fell into conversation
with other like-minded adventurers who told us the chilling story
of two climbers who fell to their death just days earlier while
climbing the south ridge. I will be honest and say this created an
uneasy feeling in the pit of my stomach. The death of a climber,
any climber, is profoundly upsetting and always unwelcome news.
But nothing, apart from the very worst the elements could throw
at us, was going to impede our objective.

The next morning we rose from our beds in plenty of time to
catch our 8am train. It was a clear day, crisp and bright and the pre-

vious evening's talk of tragedy on the Eiger was remote, not in any *sang froid* way but because we were too focused on the task ahead. We were about to take part in a hazardous game knowing only some of the potential odds which could be stacked against us like avalanches, hidden crevasses, rock falls, equipment failure, injury, illness or, a simple slip or trip on ice or loose rock which could result in a serious or even fatal accident. But, while conscious of these things they did not crowd our thoughts. Foremost in our minds was the top of the mountain – how to attain that lofty position and live to tell the tale.

On 29 January, 1991, I took the initial steps towards an historic summit. It was momentous not in any great human dramatic sense but merely because the Eiger was, and still is, regarded as one of the more illustrious Alpine challenges. But the first steps I left in the fresh snow at the foot of the mountain were indented punctuation marks on a white, featureless sheet of infinite boredom. We seemed to slog slowly under heavy packs for what seemed like an interminable period. Before long I was, to use a popular Cork expression, totally *flahed-out* (very tired), both in a physical and mental sense.

Finally, we reached the climber's shelter before the traverse to the South Col. At this point we roped together. Then with heads bent down under the sheer physical effort, we slowly and timorously made our way across a steep glacial field towards the ice-encrusted southern wall. Having traversed the glacier for almost one mile we literally froze in our footsteps when the air was cleaved by a tremendous noise like a great explosion.

'Let's get the fuck out of here, and quickly,' Littlejohn ordered, knowing instinctively that somewhere above our heads a gigantic scale of ice and snow had begun to lose its hold on the slope.

We retreated at a painfully slow pace in deep, impeding snow to the edge of the glacier. The embryonic avalanche had, fortunately, come to rest well above us but this could be a mere temporary respite. We headed back down to find a safer point at which to cross the glacier. Halfway across, having trudged about a half mile, the thunderous peal of a second settlement, or a continuation of the first, sent shock waves of sound which paralysed us with fright.

'Shit! We're halfway across. So, in either direction we run the same risk. I say let's go for it.' Again nobody disagreed with

Littlejohn. We paid out as much rope as was possible between ourselves so that if one was swept away by avalanche the remaining two would have time to dig in and act as human grapnels.

That was the theory. However we knew, deep inside, that no force on earth could withstand the force created when countless tonnes of snow and ice career down the side of a mountain. Eventually, after what seemed like an interminable period of anxious, snail-like progress, we reached the rib of snow-covered rock which, we hoped, would be our gateway to the main ridge, or arête.

'I would not like to do that again. Bloody dangerous,' said Pat looking across at the avalanche's main drag which we had somehow managed to cross without incident.

Progress was slow on the arête between the two saddles and it was here that we decided to camp down, replace the many calories consumed by our efforts and get some sleep.

'I don't believe it – my crampons have split in half, both of them. Bloody hell!' Littlejohn was decidedly disgruntled.

A crampon is as important to a climber on a snow and ice mountain as parachute to a free fall sky-diver. This posed a serious problem. Just that day while crossing a sheet of black ice I found that my crampons made little or no impression on the granite hard ice. This ridge was perilously exposed with unobstructed drops of between 2,000 and 3,000 feet on both sides.

We decided to sleep on our predicament and make a decision about whether to proceed or retreat the following morning. 'I'm just thankful this did not happen on the North Face,' were Littlejohn's last words as he dived into the warmth of his sleeping bag.

Next morning we rose with the sun. The day was cloudless with a strong wind rising. The night's rest had given us what people in Cork called *taspey* – energetic enthusiasm. This was the day we would summit, if at all. We headed across the ridge with the rope between us flapping like a clothes line in a hurricane. We were as exposed as three nudists at a tailors' convention.

After five hours of non-stop slog and grind, Littlejohn, coping with the insecurity of one crampon, made it onto the exposed rock band just below the summit. Here, on this bleak headwall, snow and ice could find no purchase due to the force of the unrelenting wind. For the next two hours my calf muscles ached from overexertion, my stomach churned due to under-nourishment and the blustering wind did its damnedest to knock me down. We eventually came upon the gradual incline of the snow field which led to the summit and I felt that odd combination of relief and fatigue.

On all sides the view was that of snow-covered, sharp and jagged mountain tops and arêtes some of which snagged wispy wads of cloud. Up here, I sensed a remote anti-climax knowing that, while we still had to climb back down, this adventure had in many respects reached its point of greatest intensity. After the traditional back slapping and mutual congratulation ceremony we tucked into a cup of water and a few squares of chocolate each and began the equally-demanding descent.

Six hours later we were still making punishingly-slow progress. Darkness had fallen and there was nowhere safe or flat enough to pitch a tent. We slept, tucked in our sleeping bags and wedged under some large, gravity-defying boulders which hung precariously on the steep face of the mountain. Needless to say, our sleep was fitful and we silently prayed the weather would not break, not now, not when we were within reach of our journey's end.

Morning popped its head above the eastern horizon and before the sun was up we devoured a hasty breakfast of the cheese, nuts and chocolate we had left in our pockets and set off. Eleven o'clock that day, after a trying and icy descent we stood on level ground. With a feeling of deep respect, we gazed back towards a mountain which, on that occasion, had allowed three men to grace its sanctified summit and return safely home to tell the tale.

The Eiger experience gave me the confidence I needed to head into the Himalaya. My apprenticeship in mountaineering was over. I had passed the final examinations and having entered the adventure sport as a novice was now carrying the knowledge given to me by my peers.

AMA DABLAM

People travel to wonder at the height of mountains, at the huge waves of the sea, at the long courses of rivers, at the vast compass of the ocean, at the circular motion of the stars ...

St Augustine

It was impossible to tell where the white granite ended and the ice began. As I viewed the spectacle from our vantage point above the Imja Khala River valley on the approach to Base Camp, I knew for certain this was the most breathtaking mountain I had ever laid eyes on. Commanding the skyline, Ama Dablam looked utterly inaccessible. This jewel in the Khumbu stood there as one of the sentinels to the greatest mountain on earth – Chomolungma.

My mind drifted back over two years of preparation to Kate Kearney's Cottage, a popular County Kerry watering hole for walkers and climbers at the Gap of Dunloe. Con and I had spent the day high on the 'Reeks and were now sitting over a pint in front of a roaring turf fire. I could tell Moriarty had something on his mind. He was unusually pensive. He devoured his pint of stout in about three thirsty gulps, turned to me and said, casually and without any hint of drama in his voice, 'What about an expedition to Ama Dablam?'

'Are you serious?' I replied, almost gagging on my drink.

'I've been going over the logistics and I think we should be able to get a decent team together for this one. It's going to take a bit of work, though, especially finding willing sponsors.'

Ama Dablam, the very name became a mantra which echoed through my mind. As I glanced at it from a distance, I realised that we were approaching one of the most monumental mountains on the face of the Earth. It easily outrivalled great European peaks like the Matterhorn and was every bit as imposing as some of the great ramparts in the Karakoram. Snow and ice covered the fang-like precipice towering above us, a sentinel of cold stone. The 6,856 metre (22,494 feet) summit radiated a hypnotic allure against a back-drop of clear blue sky.

Despite our long hours spent training and planning, a period

For the Ama Dablam team, learning First Aid included practice at injecting pain killers.

which in itself produced many thrilling adventures, I felt nothing could fully prepare a climber for the daunting task now before us. And, for the first time I began to thoroughly comprehend why so many mountaineers had been drawn to that vast arena of the Himalaya which, translated from the Sanskrit, fittingly meant 'abode of snow'.

The realisation that every other mountain we had climbed prior to this was of a distinctly lower geographical caste than any of these looming edifices had a surprisingly humbling effect on the team. No words were spoken as we each, in our own private thoughts, paid silent homage to the natural wonder which stood before us.

The Ama Dablam plan was mooted by Con in 1989. Between then and the day of our arrival in Nepal's capital, Kathmandu, in late March 1991, my thoughts, and indeed energies, focused on little else. Con was the expedition leader and fulfilled his role as strategist, motivator and, when the occasion called for it, practical joker.

Organising a major expedition is a highly stressful task. It takes long, arduous hours of sometimes brain-numbingly monotonous preparation. The success of any major climb cannot be credited to one individual. It is a team effort where every chore must be shared and those with special expertise appointed to take full responsibility in certain areas.

71

The 1991 Ama Dablam expedition team and support group.

The crew assembled under Con Moriarty's leadership for the Ama Dablam crusade were a dove-tailed bunch of lads, each of whom pulled his weight with enthusiasm. There were plenty of capable and determined shoulders to carry the weight of the planning and preparations and this allowed us each some leeway to embark on short ice-climbing sorties which became an essential part of our training.

Together, we spent much time on the Kerry mountains as well as organising trips to Scotland, England and the Alps. This ensured our stamina and fitness never fell below a critical level and helped us come to familiar terms with the nuances of each other's personality and character. And, of character, this team had plenty. Beaufort man Mike Shea, a big, strapping, long-haired and bearded young fellow with a winning demeanour; outdoor educationalist Mick Murphy, a gregarious adventurer on water and land; Tony Farrell, an experienced climber and good humoured sort; our base camp manager Tim Hickey, a Killarney walker; and Ciaran Corrigan, a wiry, quiet and reserved climber who had a fondness for the American expression 'chill out man'. Our team leader was Con 'Mountain Man' Moriarty.

Also on this trip were three friends who would trek with us as far as Base Camp – Pete Spellman, who works with a Shannon-based communications company and his wife Rose, a goldsmith, and Mick Hennessy, a helicopter pilot based in Cork. Gregarious and fun-loving, Hennessy would become one of my greatest sources of encouragement and support in the planning of my adventures.

Our journey to Ama Dablam was an exciting and ambitious expedition, especially by Irish standards. Irish mountaineering long before 1993, the year of the first successful Irish expedition to Everest, was relatively restrained in a European context. Historically, however, there have been many Irish and Anglo-Irish pioneering climbers and teams who have made their indelible mark in the log books. The North Ridge route to the top of Everest was mapped for the first time in 1920, for instance, by an expedition led by Lieutenant Colonel Howard-Bury who owned an estate near Mullingar in County Westmeath.

Among our peers, a lot of interest had been shown in what we were setting out to achieve and this placed us each under additional pressure. The feedback we got from the experienced climbing lobby was not all positive. There were many elite Irish climbers who looked upon our plan as the dream of a bunch of hopeless rookies – this was a view which they made no attempt to conceal. Nothing could divert us from following our dream. We had chosen a goal, had done our homework and had every confidence in our technical ability to cope in a high altitude environment.

In our lengthy planning debates we had agreed on a number of objectives. Getting to the top of Ama Dablam was just one, another was our desire to experience the culture of Nepal about which we had heard and read much. Coincidentally, as we were setting our sights on Ama Dablam, Belfast architect, Dawson Stelfox and Dubliner Frank Nugent, a training manager with FÁS, the Irish job training authority, were jointly leading an expedition to the 8,000 metre Manaslu, *Mountain of Soul,* in Nepal in preparation for their 1993 first Irish assault on Everest. Stelfox, Nugent and three others of the 11-strong team reached 21,000 feet, 5,000 feet shy of the top.

In the wake of this expedition, stories of deep-rooted hostility among the team members filtered through the Irish mountaineering network.

In *Everest Calling*, a book about the 1993 Everest expedition and Stelfox's successful summit attempt on 27 May of that year, the author wrote of the Manaslu outing: '... as the grains of silver gradually form a dark-room print, so a picture began to emerge from stories told in the months that followed. Stories of personal

Kathmandu, the city of a thousand temples, is a fascinating place.

initials on food bags and gas cylinders; stories of gear evicted from tents, of supplies divided to the exclusion of the support team. Stories of disagreement on tactics, on style.'

My senses crackled with the static of intense excitement as we walked from the airport through the streets of Kathmandu. Never before had I been exposed to such wondrous sights, sounds and smells. Here we were in the heart of a strange and extraordinary world about which we had only read. It was everything I thought it would be, and much more. Diverse ethnic groups, speaking different dialects and wearing strikingly distinct costumes lived together here in relative peace and harmony. Their divergent religious pursuits caused no antipathy. I could not help but wonder at the senseless bigotry which had so cruelly divided two communities living on my own island as I mingled with the welcoming dwellers of Kathmandu.

In many respects, however, this was no Shangri-la. The majority of people barely eked out a living and extreme poverty was widespread. As we made our way from the airport to our lodgings we were inundated by a rush of porters and rickshaw drivers who animatedly plied their trade in almost comical competition. Sacred cows, many of them grotesquely deformed, roamed freely through the traffic-thronged streets. These animals fed on heaps of human detritus along the footpaths. Children were everywhere, street urchins, barely old enough to walk, begged for food and money, hand-outs which for them meant life or death.

The din of the city hung in the humid and rank air. Sewage ran through open drains and into the river which cut a dirty brown gash through the city-scape. On its banks, local traders washed the fruit and vegetables which would be sold to tourists like ourselves. Outside a butcher's shop a plague of flies buzzed the offal which had been discarded in a nearby open culvert. With every turn along the labyrinth of narrow ancient streets, this bazaar of beggars, traders, hawkers, holy men, the blind and the crippled became more bizarre and alien to anything I had ever witnessed.

Kathmandu, the 'City of a Thousand Temples', is the eye of a maelstrom of religious fervour. Here could be found a myriad of houses of the holy. Surrounding these, hawkers sold brass and wood effigies of every god in the Hindu firmament. Near the temple of

A Saddhu or holy man at the temples.

Pashupatinath the effluvium became pungent with the smoke from the burning ghats, the Hindu crematoria. On the stone platforms, provided for the release of the spirit through fire, blackened and charred body parts smouldered in the still air. Camera-clicking tourists, many of whom made no attempt to conceal their utter abhorrence, were drawn to these like flying insects to the waste heaps.

Holy men were also sought out by those from the more commercially bountiful parts of the world. These people who could hardly wait to show their families and friends video images of Hindu swami like 'Milk Baba', who had a fondness for milk and whose hair was said to hold magical properties and trailed behind him like a bride's train. 'Dick Baba', who could tow a fifty-two seater bus with his penis, posed willingly with the tool of his trade exposed to the bemused on-lookers. His holy circus act, when not hauling public transport, was to lift blocks of granite which were the equivalent weight of two bags of cement.

'In Kerry, that man would never have to put his hand in his

pocket to pay for a pint,' said a gobsmacked Moriarty.

'And he'd certainly have no bother pulling one,' I replied.

From the moment of our arrival in Kathmandu anxiety, frustration and pressures triggered by myriad last minute things smashed against our resolve like flies on a windscreen. But the task was still approached with a certain degree of merriment. We were, after all, Irish climbers and wherever two or more Irish are gathered, you can be damn sure of '*a bit of craic*'.

'As I walked out from the Khumbu weeks later, my accent prompted trekkers on the Everest trail to ask if I'd anything to do with the Irish group on Ama Dablam. News travels curiously fast in the foothills of the Himalaya and the team had gained quite a reputation having the *craic* at every village to base camp,' Con Moriarty wrote in the *Irish Mountain Log*.

It was not all fun. Ama Dablam, 6,856 metres (24,494 feet), one of the most imposing peaks in the Khumbu area of Nepal, is a mountain which not so much earns respect as commands it.

'Jesus, I never thought it was that steep,' I remember Corrigan saying when we caught our first glimpse of the edifice.

The steep peak has four great ridges and four dividing faces. Satellite pictures and map images show an almost perfect cross-shaped mountain.

In the first week at Base Camp, we rested for a couple of days during which the local Buddhist priest conducted a *puja* in a bid to get the gods of the mountain on the side of the Irish.

A definite plan on all aspects of the expedition had been fought about and formulated over many pints of porter before we left home. But once there, in the shadow of our objective, all differences of viewpoint evaporated.

In our first week we established an Advance Base Camp and even managed to leave a cache of supplies on the south-west ridge leading to Camp One. Things were going really well and we were elated to be ahead of our schedule.

The ground to the ridge was a mess of huge boulders and the end of the spur was a rocky, inhospitable place with a seemingly bottomless drop down the north side to Base Camp. From that vaulted position, our tents looked like grains of black pepper on a white table cloth. Between Camp One and where we had intended to establish our next camp was a complicated and steep obstacle course of scree and boulders littered across a frighteningly-exposed ridge.

On some of the vertical sections could be seen traces of old frayed and weathered rope from earlier expeditions. Sparingly, we fixed new line where the exposure, gradient and surface posed most threat to our safety.

The climbing was the most exhilarating we had ever experienced. Huge granite blocks, towers, gullies and pinnacles coated in snow and ice lay before us as if some giant force had pounded the mountain rock into these severe formations. Our master plan was to launch the assault on the summit in teams of two – Moriarty and Shea, Murphy and Corrigan, and Farrell and myself.

Before the trekkers bade farewell, the weather, which had been calm and clear since our arrival, changed abruptly. The sky clouded over and snow began to fall. At Base Camp we sat out the snow storm in the company of other teams who were there for a similar purpose. Time was spent sitting around camp stoves drinking tea and chatting or having snow ball battles – one of the best ways of demolishing any personality barriers between teams or individuals. Violent and sudden winds, which on occasion up-rooted and

The beauty of the Himalaya unfolds as we move to Advance Base Camp.

shredded tents added to our growing angst. Seven storms unleashed their fury upon us in the course of our assault on the mountain.

On the first clear day, Moriarty and Shea, feeling strong, rested and well fed, left Base Camp for Advance Base Camp with the intention of making Camp Two the following day. That evening they sat and enjoyed a spectacular sunset over dinner. The day had gone so well and both climbers felt so fit they decided to reward themselves with a special treat – a can of pineapples which had been purchased in Kathmandu.

If Con and Mike had one thing in common, aside from their passion for climbing, it was a passion for food. These two probably preferred a juggled diet to a balanced one. Dinner, followed by dessert, followed by dinner seconds, followed by whatever was left characterised their turbo-gastronomic eating habits. But neither suspected, nor noticed, that the cherished tin of pineapples was well past its sell-by date – not until the lot had been consumed with relish, followed by more than a little regret. Twenty-four hours later they were creased by pain and suffering from the chronic vomiting and diarrhoea of severe food poisoning.

The pair were forced to retreat to Base Camp where they were glad of the 500 'quality Irish' toilet rolls packed for the trip. Mike's condition deteriorated to such an extent that it was decided necessary to get him expert medical attention at the clinic in Pheriche, a village high in the Khumbu and one day's walk from our Base Camp. Over an eight day period, he would lose a staggering two-and-a-half stone in body weight. The malady was identified as botulism. Hickey stayed with Shea while Moriarty suffered in non-silence at Base Camp with a bucket and toilet roll by his side.

Through long arduous hours fixing lines to the ice face, Corrigan and Murphy had blazed a route from Camp One to 'Yellow Tower', a massive mountainous minaret surrounded by icy, howling winds. Here, Camp Two was established at 6,092 metres (19,900 feet) and the pair returned to Base Camp.

Farrell and I intended to climb above Camp Two across punishingly poor snow and ice terrain. This was virgin territory and one of our first discoveries there was terrifyingly unexpected. Beneath a long gully we came across a climber who appeared to be sitting in the snow in all his gear looking away from Ama Dablam. It was only when we drew closer we realised this man was actually buried up to his waist and was dead. He was later identified as a Canadian climber who had perished on the mountain in a fall while abseiling in 1988, three years earlier.

Previous expeditions had reported a snow and ice gully above Camp Two which would provide steep but solid climbing for some 200 metres and provide access to the upper section of the mountain. Farrell and myself searched exhaustively for this 'doorway' but it was nowhere to be found. Instead, the huge looming face above us was a confusion of dangerous looking ice and rock above a gully devoid of snow.

We radioed Base Camp. 'Lads, there's no sign of any snow-filled couloir. Check our position with the maps and photographs. I presume we're on the right fucking mountain. Over.'

At Base Camp, nobody could quite solve the puzzle. 'Have a last look. You are positioned where you should be. Over.'

Farrell and I followed the instruction and searched again for this vital access point.

'Well fuck me! Have a look above your head Pat.'

And there, some twenty feet above the empty gully in which we stood, was a rope with a long aluminium snow stick dangling from it – an odd illustration of where the snow level had been and should have been if we were to gain access to the difficult stage above our position. We looked around for an alternative route as occasional, heavy rocks were shed by the mountain above us and crashed near where we stood.

'You wouldn't want to hang around here too long, Tony,' I remarked, throwing a nervous glance towards the dead Canadian.

To our left was a cliff which was scarred by a number of fractures. Above it, an overhang of blocks looked as if they had been pebble-dashed by a supernatural force against the side of the mountain. Tony, in a superb piece of free-style climbing lasting over two hours, scaled the cliff and took on the overhang.

Later, while traversing some mixed ground higher still, he grasped, with both hands, a huge block about the size of a large television set which smoothly came unstuck. It dropped straight towards me. I shut my eyes and heard, just above my head, the rock make contact with the steep slope. It then bounced over my head and continued its journey into the abyss below.

Shakily, we completed the work we had set out to do and fixed ropes on the most difficult section of the climb on the upper slopes.

We then returned to Camp Two, perched on the Yellow Tower. Our tents were horribly exposed here in a place too inhospitable and wind-lashed even for birds. We were the only life forms which had chosen to 'nest' here.

In the new day's light, we could see how little ground we had claimed above Camp Two the previous day. Tired and disheartened by our poor progress, we were further frustrated when a storm pinned us here for the next three days. Just before the tempest called to test our resolve, we were joined by Corrigan and Murphy who made it just before the weather closed in. For three long, endless days we remained, two in each tent, cocooned against a wind-blasted onslaught of snow. Day ran into night and night into day. We ate, dozed, read, wrote, told jokes but mainly lay there, silently waiting for the weather window to open and release us from our claustrophobic boredom.

Three days later, the sun rose above a tranquil horizon, the winds had carried their burden of snow elsewhere and Farrell and I hurriedly pushed up the mountain towards our ultimate objective, the summit. Murphy and Corrigan followed shortly behind. The sheer joy of being able to climb after three wasted days filled us with a renewed passion. We made slow progress that day and, just below Mushroom Ridge, decided to 'bivvy' for the night. With our axes Farrell and I cut a ledge, approximately seven feet by three feet and, like frozen sausage rolls inside our 'bivvy' bags, pinned ourselves with lengths of rope to our uncertain shelf.

As night progressed, we both tossed and turned fitfully as the cold penetrated our bags, clothing and bodies. The next morning I felt like a polar pupa – my breath had condensed and froze solid during the night forming a one inch thick seal of ice over the opening of the bag. I had to break this icy lid in order to stick my head through.

The morning looked bright and promising but our bags were quite wet, too wet to be of any use to us another night higher on the mountain. After a hasty breakfast, Tony and I decided to drop to Base Camp to rest for a day or two, proud at having achieved this lofty perch and still left with plenty of time and energy with which to launch another assault. Another night spent high on the mountain with wet sleeping bags was, we reckoned, a recipe for frostbite, if nothing else.

As we left our 'bivvy' site, Mick and Ciaran, who had spent

their night 150 feet below us in a snow cave, continued their ascent along the heavily-corniced Mushroom Ridge, where each footfall had to be carefully placed on the unstable snow. At the end of this fatiguing scramble along the ridge the two climbers, who were travelling light, bivouacked comfortably in the snow for their second night.

The previous day, Ciaran felt unwell but believed this was a temporary problem and felt that he would recover overnight. The following morning was cold and bitter. Both climbers awoke intending this to be their summit day. However, within a few minutes of moving around, Ciaran realised he was not fit to attempt the summit. Both discussed the options over breakfast. The climbers were torn, and after some debate, Ciaran said, 'Murphy, you go for the summit. I must go down.' Neither climber could foresee the consequences of their decision.

Ciaran made radio contact with Base Camp and told Moriarty of his predicament. From the description of his suffering it was apparent to us all that Ciaran was the victim of acute mountain sickness. Con asked Ciaran to put Mick on the open radio.

'Murphy's ... not here. He's ... gone ... for the summit,' came his reply.

The expression on the faces of all who heard the message from Ciaran was one of concern. Corrigan was on his own and had begun his perilous and staggering descent along the exposed ridge, a challenge for any able-bodied climber.

Meanwhile, Murphy continued to climb as scales of ice fell 5,000 feet below him to the Mingbo glacier. Our earlier feelings towards him gave way to one of spiritual support as we watched him through telescope and binoculars cross the bergschrund. Murphy was making his bid for the summit.

As Moriarty would later write in the *Irish Mountain Log*, 'he was like a lone fly on a huge tapestry – steadily moving up'. His progress was achingly slow to all those who watched through telescopes and binoculars from Base Camp.

At 5.30pm on 4 April, 1991, Mick reached the top of Ama Dablam. He planted our country's Tricolour, set a national mountaineering record for the team and enjoyed the views. He was the highest Irishman on Earth.

As Mick progressed towards the summit, Con set out for Camp One where he met Ciaran, now in the company of some American climbers who were giving him hot broth. After resting and eating, Ciaran continued down towards Base Camp on his own, drawn by the prospect of oxygen. Con continued across the ridge to Camp Two towards Murphy. About 100 metres below Advance Base Camp Ciaran met Ben Schriffen, an American doctor, who urged him to continue his descent. Shortly before Base Camp two sherpas, en route to his assistance, met him and accompanied him down. On arrival, he was met by myself and Tony, who were shocked at his pallor. His physical appearance bore no resemblance to that of 36 hours earlier.

That night, Ben Schriffin, part of a US team which failed to make it to the summit, decided the prognosis was good. Ciaran had dropped to low altitude soon enough to avoid permanent physiological damage or even death. Two days later, when Murphy victoriously hobbled, frost-bitten, into Base Camp, Ciaran had already made some positive recovery and the worst hours of his illness were behind him. In the words of Moriarty, 'the initial anger and frustration that had been felt by a number of team members was dissipated by an overpowering sense of achievement'.

Everybody, especially our American neighbours at Base Camp, had been extremely worried for Corrigan and Murphy's safe return. Now, the sense of great relief spread through the camp leaving no soul untouched. Champagne and wine bottles were uncorked and we toasted what was, in fact, the only summit success on Ama Dablam that particular season. For thirty days and through seven ferocious storms, we had struggled to briefly claim the summit of Ama Dablam.

This expedition will always stand out in my mind as being my first experience in a so-called Third World country. On a mountain sacred to the native people, with a close-knit bunch of friends, I learned the importance of team work. The effects of high altitude and the extremes of weather on big mountains were valuable lessons which we all learned.

RETURN TO KATHMANDU

There's a race of men that don't fit in,
A race that can't stay still;
So they break the hearts of kith and kin
And they roam the world at will
They range the field and they rove the flood
And they climb the mountain's crest.
Theirs is the curse of the gypsy blood
And they don't know how to rest.

Robert Service

As I walked out of the Khumbu I turned one last time to gaze back in awe at Ama Dablam. I felt then that I too possessed the same spiritual umbilical cord connection which Sherpas believe will always draw them back to the Himalaya. It had been my first experience at high altitude on a mountain which was deeply respected in the uppermost echelon of mountaineers. Had it not been for the inclement weather I knew deep inside that I could have, I would have, made the summit in the wake of Mick Murphy's thrilling climb.

I had gone to the Himalaya with the romantic idea that I might, to use an American expression, 'find myself'. The experience left me changed in many ways, though I could not be certain that it had opened some direct line of communication with my inner self.

On my return home, it became painfully obvious that my passion for climbing and the reconstruction of my business was taking its toll on my wife. Marie and I had reached a stage where the rift between us became too great to bridge and we decided to go our separate ways.

I rented a flat on Patrick's Hill with a commanding view of Cork city. For the next two years, I spent every spare moment hill walking or climbing with my rapidly-expanding coterie of like-minded friends and acquaintances. With some of these I shared what had been until then a deep-rooted desire – my intention to climb Everest.

This was a decision I reached the last day I glanced at Ama

83

Mark Miller, who had a burning desire to climb Everest, but died in a pre-expedition plane crash.

Dablam and saw in the Himalayan distance the white plume of cloud which flew like a Buddhist prayer flag from the lofty peak of Chomolungma. There and then, I knew I would one day stand on her summit.

At home, I searched to find an Everest team I could join. There was an all-Irish expedition being planned for the spring of 1993 under the joint leadership of Frank Nugent and Dawson Stelfox. A well-organised concern, this group included some of the most accomplished climbers in the country. The expedition generated a high public profile and secured blanket media coverage and substantial State, private and corporate sponsorship.

By the time I made contact with the team leaders they had already assembled a full complement of climbers. Deeply disappointed I nonetheless understood that not all dreams become an immediate reality.

Undeterred, I sought alternative options. Lady luck smiled on me when on a climbing trip to Scotland. There I encountered a 28 year-old English climber, Mark Miller, whose dream coincided with mine. He was planning a journey to the north face of Everest and when he heard of my predicament, invited me to join his expedition. Mark and I became friendly and I looked forward to joining his expedition team. The climb would be executed under the aegis of Mark's adventure holiday company – Out There Trekking. But, as this was his first major adventure, he was more focused on succeeding than making a commercial profit. This was good news for me. Normally, an Everest climb could cost anything up to US$45,000 but my required investment in this undertaking was just US$15,000.

Tragically, Mark never made it to Everest. He died in an horrific air crash while flying over the Himalaya on a reconnaissance flight in preparation for our journey. Our expedition would be dedicated to his memory.

During most of a self-imposed two-year break – during which I did keep in regular contact with Marie and the boys – I diligently prepared for the expedition.

On the business front, I found myself working less and less on 'the line' as a mason and devoting more time to the establishment of an auctioneering firm and mortgage brokerage. Money, the accumulation of which had once been the main driving force in my life, was now of peripheral importance only. On the mountains and hills, I saw no sense in paying homage to Mammon when nothing could purchase, or compare to the priceless wealth of what Nature had to offer all those willing to open their hearts.

I never considered climbing to be my way of running away from the harsh realities of life. The hills and mountains provided the environment in which I could meditate deeply and solve my problems. From the time I was 15 years of age I had followed an unwavering course, with no concept of the wide and wonderful world that existed outside my small, confined habitat. Climbing for me opened up new horizons and presented windows through which I have been able to gaze at some of the many diverse cultures and peoples which inhabit our earth. It has been a continuous learning process and an education for which I will always be thankful. Taking on big mountains has not just been a physical trial. There is the cultural element, but it also represents man's atavistic desire to pit himself against the forces of nature and his inner self. Mountains enabled me to find peace and tranquillity and an undeniable element of escapism from the negative forces to which, as a successful businessman, I had so willingly subjected myself.

At 10.07am on 27 May, 1993, Dawson Stelfox, the Belfast architect and mountain guide, became the first Irishman to reach the summit of Mount Everest and, as a dual passport holder, Stelfox also became the first Briton to climb the mountain by the extremely dangerous North Ridge, following the footsteps of Mallory and Irving. On his return home, I rang Stelfox to offer my warmest congratulations to him and each member of the first Irish Everest expedition team, including my Ama Dablam team mate, Mick

Murphy.

The summer of 1993 drew to a close and I became very conscious of two intensifying sensations. Firstly, the rising anticipation of the Everest expedition, which had been scheduled for that autumn, and secondly a desire to be reunited with my family as I approached this momentous milestone. Two weeks prior to my departure for Kathmandu, after a number of reconciliatory discussions with Marie, I moved back into the family home. The support of my family and close friends was for me an essential prerequisite.

Thoughts of death on Everest crept in and out of my consciousness. I knew the risks involved, especially above the 8,000 metres (26,000 feet) line, the so-called 'death zone' where the levels of oxygen in the atmosphere were insufficient to support life for long periods of time. The evening before I was to fly out and join twenty-two climbers from Nepal, Australia, Finland, France, Russia, Poland, the United States and Britain, I was looking after last minute preparations and listening to the radio when a world news item chilled me to the very marrow.

The worst monsoon weather to strike Nepal and Tibet in over forty years had caused rivers to burst through their banks, mud slides had wiped out entire villages and 4,000 people had lost their lives. I could not believe what I was hearing. Our expedition had been carefully scheduled to kick-in at the close of the monsoon season but Mother Nature was not quite finished and the seasonal deluge was still wreaking havoc.

Hoping that things, on the weather front, would improve we pressed ahead with our plans. I was glad we had decided to persevere as a cancellation would have been impossible to imagine after so long a period of training and agonising fundraising for the trip. Despite my best efforts, I had failed to find a major commercial sponsor for the trip. Through hard work and with the help of my supportive friends we could only drum-up two-thirds of the finance needed for the venture. Much of the monies I raised came via slide show talks to climbing and walking groups throughout Ireland and donations from a number of small businesses.

In the wake of one of these talks at University College, Cork (UCC) I encountered a man who was to become one of my closest friends, secondary school-teacher and devout hillwalker Joe O'Leary. In the course of our initial conversation, Joe and I found we had a lot in common as well as our passion for the outdoor life.

The worst monsoon in forty years caused mass destruction.

Joe's family had farmed and lived at Tower, Blarney which was not very far from my home and we both drank in the same local.

Some weeks after the UCC lecture, Joe and I headed off on our first foray together. By the close of that day's walking it was obvious that a solid friendship and great affinity had been forged between us. With an imperturbable manner and astuteness, Joe was to become one of the main supports of my seven summit plan and together we would later climb, not once but twice, to the top of Africa's Kilimanjaro, 5,895 metres (19,340 feet).

I knew none of the climbers in the Everest team but the support I received at home during training as well as the more bureaucratic preparations were something I never took for granted. This more than made up for the possible lack of moral support I anticipated on Everest.

My biggest concern, prior to my departure, was the extended monsoon season which Joe and I discussed the evening before my departure as we checked and double checked my inventory.

At the airport the following morning I bade farewell to my family and a few close friends at the boarding gate. As I turned to bid a final farewell, my mother, with tears welling in her eyes, pressed a holy medal into my hand. 'May God protect you, Pat,' she wept, fearful that she might not see me again.

During the lengthy flight to Kathmandu I slept little. My mind was in a state of high anxiety. This was it, the first leg of my journey to the top of the world and to the mountain of my dreams. Facts and figures regarding Chomolungma ran frenziedly through my consciousness like a pack of data-filled runaway fairground bumper cars.

'The highest mountain on Earth is known to the native peoples who live in its shadow as Chomolungma, meaning "Goddess Mother" of the Earth,' said the tour guide inside my head.

'Everest is 29,028 feet above sea level. It commands one of the most impressive chains of mountains on Earth, known as The Himalaya. Himalaya is a Sanskrit word meaning "abode of snow".

'The geological origin of these mountains, which run from Afghanistan to Burma and along the way dominate regions such as Pakistan, Sikim, Kashmir, Northern India, Southern China, Nepal, Tibet and Bhutan, is almost beyond man's comprehension. Fossil remains of sea creatures have been found on these mountains above the 8,000 metres (26,000 feet) line.

'Where did these mountains come from? Scientists say that millions of years ago the great sub-continent of India was an island which travelled northwards some 5,000 km from southern latitudes to crash into the Eurasian continent. This collision created a crumbling of the Earth's crust and pushed the mountains upwards in an accordion-like movement.

'Over 150 of the Himalayan peaks are higher than any other mountain on Earth.

'The people who live in the fertile valleys between the foothills of the Himalaya include diverse ethnic groups, the Balti, Sherpa, Gurung among many others – each with their own customs, language and religion. All of these peoples have one thing in common – their adoration of the mountains, the abode of their gods.

'The first Westerners to venture into the Himalaya did so in 1885 and from that time a furious debate raged for some decades as to whether or not Everest could be climbed.

'Many attempts were made to climb the mountain, especially at the turn of the twentieth century. To this day mystery surrounds the British expedition which included George Mallory and Andrew Irvine.

'In June, 1924 these two climbers disappeared above 8,000 metres (26,500 feet). When last sighted, through a break in the clouds, by their colleagues high on the mountain, these two pioneers of mountaineering were making their way to the summit.

Did they achieve that goal? Nobody knows, as they never returned.

'The first Westerner to climb the mountain was New Zealand bee-keeper Edmund Hillary who, in the company of Sherpa Tenzing Norkay, summited on May 29, 1953.'

'Excuse me, Sir. We are about to land. Could you please fasten your seat-belt,' said the stewardess bringing me back to reality.

The frantic pace, jarring traffic din and multitudinous aromas of Kathmandu were just as I remembered them. Once outside the main doors of the airport each step I took was one closer to my all-consuming goal. Everest was no longer inside my head but almost

Tsiring Bhim Bhandur, a sherpa who remains a close friend.

within my grasp. The warm rain and extreme humidity soaked me seconds after leaving the cover of the airport terminal. Into every life a little rain must fall but things were going to be difficult enough without this extended monsoon season.

At the airport I was greeted by my Nepalese friend, Tsiring Bhim Bhandur, a 23 year-old Sherpa I had first met in 1991 and who since had lived with me in Cork for a period of time where he quickly became one of the family.

'Hello, Mr Pat. Welcome back to Kathmandu – just like Ireland, isn't it?' he joked, looking skywards at the rain-saturated clouds.

'Yeah Tsiring, it's a nice soft day alright.'

A swarm of airport porters decended on my bags like mosqui-toes. Each fought against the other to secure the business of carry-ing my bags for a few rupees. Tsiring, with highly animated instructions, ushered them away – he had brought his cousin Prim to help me with the baggage. A taxi was hailed to take us to Tsiring's home, a small, two-roomed apartment in the suburbs. For the next week I would live with this extraordinary man, his wife and child, whom, influenced by his Irish sojourn, he called Mike Bhim Bhandur.

Tsiring, five feet four inches in height, of slim build and good looks, ran fifteen miles every day as part of a strict exercise regime. He had been an Asian kick-boxing champion who, in the course of his competitive bouts, had killed five opponents. A climber of many Himalayan peaks, he had been married at twelve years of age, not unusual among the Sherpas, and divorced at seventeen. He remarried a beautiful young woman called Bisnu who was carrying his second child whom he would call Mary Bhim Bhandur.

During that week with Tsiring he took me an an exploratory tour of his homeland during which we visited many of the historical and cultural places of interest in Kathmandu and the surrounding valleys. In the company of Prim, Tsiring and I went on a solemn five-day trek to the place where Mark Miller had perished the previous year.

Returning to Kathmandu, Tsiring received bad news. His sister-in-law had been killed in a landslide near Jiri and he was summoned to assist the family with the funeral arrangements.

Eager to meet the other climbers I headed for the hotel. Once inside the door an almost electric air of excitement radiated from the team members assembled there. Introductions were made but it would be many days yet before the automatic and reflexive sizing-up process by each member of the other members would gather momentum. Of the group, a cocktail of nationalities, I already knew seven with whom I had climbed.

The next morning I awoke early to the sound of the incessant rain drumming against my hotel bedroom window. A hasty breakfast was consumed and, with all the excited animation of a bunch of school children going on a day trip, we loaded our gear onto a convoy of trucks and four-wheel-drive vehicles. These would snake their way north eastwards to the border of Nepal and Tibet and into the bosom of the Great Himalayan Range.

The impact of the deluge on the landscape and people was horrendous. Our train of vehicles made hesitant progress as we encountered landslide after landslide blocking the treacherous roadway above the gorges of the swollen and visibly angry rivers cutting deep and jagged scars through the land. We witnessed the plight and desperation of the natives – as many as 4,000 would drown in distended torrents of white water or smother under flash mud slides during this one monsoon season. Outbreaks of dysentry and related illnesses took their toll also.

I felt like some cold-blooded interloper who had come here not to ease their plight but to pit myself against forces which these welcoming Tibetans and Nepalese knew could never be conquered.

Beyond Lamosangu we crossed the Sun Kosi river which created an ominous gorge into which I expected the track to collapse at any moment sending our caravan careering down into the flood waters. From this point onwards we made 'two steps forward, one step back' progress. Huge boulders, as big as Volkswagen vans, stood stubbornly in our path. We abandoned the trucks and hired porters to take us on foot to the next clear stretch of roadway where we managed, somehow, to hire some replacement vehicles to carry our tonnes of food and equipment to our 'trek-Tatapannie' – acclimatisation trek and starting point.

Over the next ten days we arduously pushed our way to 5,500 metres in a bid to get our bodies acclimatised to high altitude and carry out a final check on our fitness status. At high altitude the physiological functions of the human body, no matter how well tuned, undergo utter changes. The level of blood haemoglobin, that miracle of biology which transports oxygen through the body, increases in order to counteract the effects of the rarefied environment. The heart and lungs expand to cater for high altitude-stress. It is virtually impossible to tell how any person will react to this radical change in living conditions.

I lay in my tent during those first days of the trek reading medical articles on the effects of high altitude sickness. Not exactly bedtime reading but I wanted to be the first to realise if, at any stage, my body found the going too tough and, more especially, the air too thin.

The three primary physiological threats are pulmonary oedema, cerebral oedema or thrombosis. And, each and every one of these sounded positively catastrophic.

Pulmonary oedema: the oxygen in your lungs is not sufficient to keep the fluids of your body out of your lungs, fluids from the cells leak into the spaces between the cells and you drown in your own fluids, read the blood-chilling blurb to one of the articles.

Cerebral oedema: fluids leak from cells in your brain and this causes abnormal swelling, which in turn can cause death. Oh! bollocks, I

The main road from Nepal to Tibet blocked by landslides.

thought, as if the threat of falling into a crevasse or being buried
under an avalanche was not bad enough I now had the additional
worry of my head filling up like a water balloon.

That was not all. *Thrombosis: due to the increase in red blood cells
your blood thickens and can form a clot in a blood vessel or in the heart
and cause death.*

I lay back on the camp bed and listened to the rain on the canvas. It made a drumming sound like that of a demented bodhran
player. Before quenching the light I conducted a final leech patrol
of my body. For the past number of days, ever since the trek began,
the entire group had been plagued by these blood-sucking worms
which would alight on arms and legs and torso with no hint of
their presence. The weather conditions had caused an explosion in
their population and it was impossible to avoid the ubiquitous par-
asites. At night, as we slept, armies of these annoying little creatures would enter through a myriad of chinks they somehow managed to find in our tents. This upset quite a few members of the
expedition who feared that these worms could carry the deathly
HIV virus associated with AIDS.

One morning, I awoke to discover one stuck to my throat, like
a vampire's medium. It was bloated with blood which it had
sucked from my body all night long.

'Oh Jesus Christ!' I cried as I hurriedly rushed around my tent
looking for the salt canister as the fat, black, slug-like animal clung
to my throat. In old Hollywood movies, a burning cigarette end is

often used by actors to rid themselves of leeches. Once the burning tobacco made contact with the worm it released its suction hold. I am not a smoker and, even if I was, I do not know if I would try this method. We found a liberal sprinkle of salt was enough to per-suade the bloodsucker to release its hold. The almost reflexive reaction is to pull the damn thing off but, while the bite is painless, this causes the wound to bleed for a considerable time afterwards.

It rained for between ten and twenty hours a day for the dura-tion of the trek. It was ten days of pure misery but an acid test of the patience, resolve and sheer determination of our team. The spirits of each and every one of us lifted to a higher plane when it was time to head back to the border and make our way to Tibet and our Everest Base Camp.

With great relief we made our way to Kodari where the next leg of our journey would begin. This, we hoped, marked the end of leech infestation and the monotonous monsoon.

EVEREST MARK ONE

I suppose we go to Everest ... because we can't help it. Or, to state the matter rather differently, because we are mountaineers. Our case is not unlike that of one who has, for instance, a gift for music. There may be inconvenience, and even damage, to be sustained in devoting time to music; but the greatest danger is in not devoting enough, for music is this man's adventure.

Mallory

If asked to describe the most dangerous part of an expedition to the roof of the world, I would have to think long and hard before uttering a response. Then, I would probably say the journey to the Everest Base Camp can be fraught with more perilous and unexpected danger than any found on the actual climb.

We had left our last trekking camp and were loaded back into an assortment of trucks and jeeps which were to take us over the Chinese border and, eventually, to Everest Base Camp. The mood of the expedition was one of sheer elation as the road climbed ever higher and we prayed the monsoon rains would finally ease. We drove through ramshackle settlements made more pitiful by rains which turned the earth into a filthy brown and congealed ooze which ran from the hillsides covering every trail and route throughout the weather-wasted landscape.

The team's feeling of exultation fell face first into a pile of bureaucratic bullshit when we encountered the first Chinese border guards. These stony-faced officials are as unlike the native Nepalese and Tibetan peoples as it is possible to imagine. Their faces exhibit no more expression than could be found in the countenance of a fish. Had it not been for the diplomatic aplomb of our liaison officer and interpreter, we would still be stuck in the border town of Zhangmu trying to satisfy the outrageous demands of these Chinese public servants. The border guards went through our papers with a serious disdain normally reserved for an army of invasion.

After what seemed like an interminable period of the ancient Chinese hair-splitting ceremony, we were given the necessary

94

stamps of officialdom in order to proceed.

The delayed journey from Zhangmu to Base Camp was more terrifying and thrilling than any I could have imagined. The fun, which I can now safely call it, began just outside Zhangmu on the way to Nyalam, one of the most aptly named places in the universe. In translation it roughly means 'road to hell' and nothing, even in Dante's imagination could have been more spot-on.

The truck in which I travelled was a rolling, noisy, rattling illustration of the miracle of gravity. How it managed to stay on this one-lane roadway of loose rubble, mud and boulders with a sheer fall of hundreds of feet into the deep gorge flanking one side, is something I will never be able to comprehend. I still get an icy shiver through the core of my spine when I think of the drop to the side of the road where surface ended abruptly and air began.

My hands clamped the frame of the seat like a drowning man's hold on a life-belt. Nothing on the mountain, I thought, could be more horrific than this. Is it any wonder that almost half of the serious accidents during Everest expeditions occur while groups are en route to the mountain? I tried hard to banish all thoughts of the potential threat to life and limb being created by this truck trip to hell and, instead, allowed each adrenalin rush at the treacherous road bends to produce a feeling of excitement. The mind is like a dog – it has to be trained and disciplined. And in this instance I commanded mine to be full of *joie de vivre* rather than scared shitless terrified.

After passing Nyalam the landscape took on the majestic panorama of the high Tibetan plateau. It looked, in every respect, like not only the abode of snow but also the abode of the Buddhist deities. It is a barren land, though geologically magnificent. Stone and mud symmetrical farm houses made from the same fabric as the surrounding landscape were poignant proof of man's ability to eke out a living here in what to my eyes was a place where life could not be sustained.

All the people we met on the road to Everest, apart from the obstinate Chinese border guards, were not in the least bit envious of our gross affluence in comparison to their few material possessions. Smiling, though malnourished children with matted hair and thread-bare clothes, ran excitedly alongside our convoy whenever we passed through the tiny hamlets which punctuated the vast remoteness of this tortured landscape.

Tibetan children are invariably smiling.

As the road through the foothills of the Himalaya wound through each high pass I longed to catch our first glimpse of Chomolungma. There was no view and a slate grey monsoon sky covered the mountains with a dense cloak through which no image of our objective could escape.

Many climbing seasons on Everest had, in the recent past, been total wash-outs and I began to feel a sense of despondency as we drew ever closer to the cloud-smothered mountains.

At 5,200 metres (17,000 feet) our climbing circus drove through the pass at Pang La, portal to the most majestic range of mountains on earth. I gazed longingly to the south but all I could see was the rain-laden backdrop of dense cloud.

Some hours later we arrived at the Buddhist monastery of Rongbuk nestled in the lap of the mountain gods. The gracious and welcoming monks, who in appearance really looked no different from their yak-herding, lay brethren, except for their brightly coloured clothing, showed no outward signs of the brutal regime imposed by the Chinese forces of occupation since the 1950s.

Tibetans have long suffered under Chinese oppression. It saddened me to think that so many like these gentle, loving and devoted Buddhist monks and nuns had been murdered and tortured by the invaders, who in many parts of Tibet out-number the indigenous people by three to one. In the 1960s, over seven million Chinese were settled as part of the sinister plan to obliterate the Tibetan culture. The result of this has been the demotion to 'second class citizen' of Tibetan natives who have become subjugated by the Chinese settlers.

The western world has largely ignored the plight of these

unique people whose very identity, heritage and spirituality is being bloodily erased from the pages of modern civilisation. The atrocities committed against these inherently peaceful folk are every bit as hellish as those associated more recently with the conflict in Cambodia with Pol Pot.

Coming from a country whose language, the life-blood of any culture, was suppressed along with our political identity for hundreds of years by an occupational force and which remains divided and in turmoil to this day, I felt I had a deeper understanding of the pain these people have to endure under China's strangle-hold. These considerations had me questioning again the morality of credit card expeditions to countries where people endure a lifelong struggle to survive. I tried to reconcile myself with the fact that we brought much-needed currency to the region and, were it not for non-blinkered visiting westerners, the brutality of the Chinese might be far worse than it is.

The Rongbuk Glacier Base Camp was established on a huge flat table of frozen and snow-crusted ochre mud. Our gear was off-loaded and stored in the many tents which looked as if they were floating on the surface of a huge snow-covered lake. Prayer flags, like bunting, hung wet and limp above the camp as visiting monks performed their traditional blessing of our exploit.

That first evening, as we sat in the mess tent, I looked at the bearded and weathered faces around the table and wondered why the lofty peaks of mountains should be such an opiate to so many different people. We were some assemblage of climbing all-sorts. Twenty-three individuals, one as interesting as the next, from all walks of life and each one a stimulating personality. Maciej Berbeka, the Pole, who had already climbed on five of the 8,000-metre peaks; Norman Croucher whose legs had been amputated below the knees and Nish Bruce who, at some later date, was planning to do a parachute jump from 130,000 feet, at the border of space. Also there was Brigitte Muir, who was endeavouring to complete her seven summit challenge with her husband John, a renowned Australian adventurer who had already added Everest to his impressive list of conquests. Nish Bruce, Harry Taylor and Dr Karl Heinze, an ex-NASA astronaut, were intending to measure atmospheric radiation on Everest as part of the design project for Nish's historic jump-suit.

I took an instant liking to a smiling, almost constantly smoking,

Russian speed climber, George Kotov. Like myself, George had climbed expedition mountains throughout the world and had an insatiable love of adventure, of big mountains and living on the edge.

For the next week the weather played havoc with our plans. It snowed every day causing our frustration to pile up. We could do little else but sit and wait for the weather to improve. My time spent tent-bound was not fruitless however. The interaction with these people from all quarters greatly stimulated me. With these global campers I discussed political, environmental and diverse social issues. This stirred deeper interests and a longing to learn more about other races, other cultures.

One endless and monotonous day followed another as we remained bogged-down in Rongbuk slush for a full week. I awoke suddenly one morning and something was different. Then it dawned on me, literally, when a clear light penetrated the fabric of my tent. I hurriedly dressed and emerged to join those who had met the sunrise before me.

'There's a break in the weather, Pat,' said George, through a miniature cumulus of smoke from his first cigarette of the day.

I paid little heed. My eyes were held fast by the splendour of the snow-dusted giants which stood proud and high above a cummerbund of cloud. Chomolungma, the Goddess, had decided to grant us an audience, albeit a distant one.

Furious immediacy threw the team into action. We had decided to take full advantage of this long-awaited break in the weather. Enthusiastic chatter mingled with the gentle ringing of yak bells. Personality differences were cast aside and the team came together this morning as one united force with a common and now visible objective – the highest mountain.

The group was divided into three. I found myself with George, Maciej Barbeka, Frenchman Thierry Renard, John and Brigitte Muir and John Tinker. Quiet and reserved, Tinker took over the leadership of the expedition following the death of Mark Miller. Tinker was a man who easily won the respect of other climbers due to his infectious discipline and professionalism.

Our target was to proceed in a caravan of 30 yaks to Advance Base Camp at 21,000 feet with three Sherpas, Ang Babu, Lharpa – two high altitude climbers – and Ang Rita, our Sirdar and chief cook.

As I took those first enthusiastic steps up the tail end of the Rongbuk glacier, little did I realise the depth of misery and tragedy which lay before me.

For three days we slogged onwards and upwards through snow which rarely became more than ankle deep. The time spent at Base Camp piling on the calories did not provide the energy boost I was expecting. The higher we climbed the greater the effort became. It was obvious acclimatisation would not be achieved without some considerable effort. In three days we had covered fourteen miles of the glacier, gaining 1,200 metres (4,000 feet). Fully adjusted to high altitude, a climber could cover this much ground in under ten hours.

There was little conversation between us on the final day's approach to Advance Base Camp. My lungs heaved with every breath I took but my anguish was no different from that of my team mates. Arriving at Advance Base Camp, 6,400 metres (21,000 feet), tired and finding it hard to breathe, we set up our most important camp site since the whole adventure began.

Yaks moving from Base to Advance Base Camp.

Here, the level of oxygen in the air was less than half that which our bodies required. Most of our energy was spent merely breathing.

From this point upwards we would burn in the order of 6,000 calories per day while only having a daily intake of 2,000 calories – the ultimate diet. In six weeks I lost three-and-a-half stone (forty-nine pounds) body weight.

Over the next number of days we awaited the gradual arrival of the remainder of the team and some sixty yak-loads of food and gear. Our leader, Jon Tinker, had decided to orchestrate the expedition from Base and Advance Base Camp.

We had entered the most dangerous part of the expedition. From here on we had to be ever mindful of the risks – avalanches, frostbite, cold, high jet-stream winds and high-altitude sickness.

The damage which wind chill can almost instantly cause to man's fragile cellular fabric was made terrifyingly clear to us in the following weeks when two Indian climbers arrived off the mountain into our Advance Base Camp. The expression of horror in their faces said it all. They had made it to 7,600 metres (25,000 feet) in fairly clear conditions. But with the weather window about to close they took some photographs from their lofty perch below the austere summit of Chomolungma. For reasons which neither of them could rationalise they removed their layered gloves to take the snap-shots. In seconds one received severe frostbite on seven fingers, the other had damaged four fingers in the high jet-stream winds. The digits were painfully swollen and looked like black and blue rolls of putrefying meat. Both men would lose some fingers as a result of their ill judgement.

It snowed incessantly at Advance Base Camp for the next few days, most of which was spent in our tents becoming accustomed to high altitude. By now the entire team had assembled and the level of pent-up frustration became an almost tangible quality. Quiet men became aggressive, patient men became impatient and those with short tempers became manic. Obviously nobody wanted to spend this much time at our first advance position and it showed. The want, the need, to put our foot on the mountain after years of planning and preparation became all-consuming. But, Everest has no mercy on those who disregard her warnings. Patience was the key to our survival – we had to sit and wait, and wait.

After just over seven more days of obstructive weather, the break we had all been eager for came. The decision was immediate – the push towards the top would begin as quickly as we could pack our rucksacks.

The sunlight was reflected on every surface of the mountain and the combination of direct and reflected ultra violet rays caused the flaking skin on my face to become as tight as a bodhran drum. Sun block reduced the sore effects of the weathering but not totally.

It was punishingly hard work making the climb from Advance Base Camp north-east along the East Rongbuk Glacier to the infamous North Col. My lungs gasped for air like a pair of overworked mechanical bellows.

The North Col umbilical cord linking Everest to Changtse, 7,583 metres (24,878 feet) looked monumental. This section of the mountain is especially prone to avalanche and claimed the highest death toll. The frozen snow rose before me creating what looked like a sheer wall. High above the North Col looked both welcoming and intimidating.

We struggled wearily, ever conscious of the threat of the snow's instability. Each glance to the Col above was accompanied by thoughts of countless thousands of tonnes of snow suddenly deciding to follow the laws of gravity and come thundering and roaring down the steep and enormous chute between us and it. The daily falls of snow made conditions less than ideal.

We decided to fix ropes in position such was the perilousness of the underfoot conditions. Even the points of my crampons failed to bite where the light snow lay powdered over a permafrosted layer. A slip here and you would become a human toboggan on a multi thousand-feet death ride.

On arrival at the North Col I felt as elated and relieved as though we had reached the summit. Tents were pitched at Camp One, 7,060 metres (23,000 feet) at the foot of the imposing North Ridge. At last we were making progress. From here, weather permitting, the top of the mountain could be reached with the establishment of two further camps – one at 7,900 metres and the final one at the 8,300 metres (27,000 feet) mark.

As soon as we had unpacked our gear and stashed most of it inside the small, lightweight dome tents, the stoves were ignited to melt snow and provide the liquids so necessary to avoid dehydration. The following day we descended all the way back down to Base Camp to recover from our efforts at high altitude.

While I rested with some of the team at Base Camp, other members of the team were stocking-up Camp One. A few days well-earned rest and we were on the move again having now become fairly well acclimatised.

For the next five weeks, we would pay many visits to our lofty perch at the North Col. We had retreated to Base Camp, the chain having been put in place linking Base to Advance Base Camp and Camp One, the springboard to the upper reaches of the mountain.

The dream which had permeated both my sleeping and waking hours was, I felt, about to be realised.

TRAGEDY ON EVEREST

I'm not a failure because I didn't make it ...
I'm a success because I've tried.

Anonymous

It was as if the lightweight dome tent in which I sheltered had been picked up by some giant pair of hands which were now kneading it into a distorted shape. The poles, which were no thicker than my small finger and over which the thin synthetic fabric was stretched, barely withstood the fearful force which bent them out of shape. I was trapped inside this bombarded bubble while outside the wind sounded like the roar of an airplane engine at full throttle.

The earth is said to be wrapped in some 5,600 million tonnes of air and here, at Camp Two, 7,907 metres (25,900 feet), I was beginning to feel that most of it was now being dumped with great might against our only protection from the wrath of Chomolungma.

We were plagued by almost daily falls of snow as we struggled to gain even higher ground. Our route to the North Ridge took us on one of the most featureless sections of high altitude mountain anyone could set a cramponed foot on. This enormous ridge was covered with snow on its leeward side. Where the winds had full vent, the dark skeletal rock of the mountain lay exposed. We climbed on the snow ridge not far from where it met the precipitous rock and, with each step, prayed that it held fast. An avalanche here, even a relatively small one in terms of tonnage, would have had fatal consequences.

There were many times when I felt walking up this snow and ice was beyond the capability of mortal man as I gasped for air along every step of the way. We moved slowly, ever conscious of the fact that the slope was in poor condition and a slip here, on the ridge, would send a climber plummeting to certain death.

At Camp Two, we hastily erected our tents and made some hot drinks. From this point upwards, I never paid too much attention to the food we ate, which was mostly concentrated carbohydrate, high energy biscuits and the occasional chocolate treat. I consumed these rations not expecting any taste sensation but merely to maintain my calorie level. Eating, like breathing, became a totally subconscious bodily function. Sleeping was another matter. Here, with so little oxygen in the air, we were all quietly concerned about the effects of oxygen depletion. As yet, none of us had resorted to using the oxygen bottles, so vital for the final onslaught on the summit.

During my first night at Camp Two, I spent two hours melting snow on the stove to rehydrate my body after the punishing climb during which every single atom of my body was placed under excruciating pressure. At 8pm that evening, feeling thoroughly exhausted, I worked my way into my high altitude thermal sleeping bag, making sure I had my plastic pee bottle to avoid having to crawl outside to answer nature's call. I closed my eyes and fell into a deep, blank and dreamless sleep. When I awoke it was 3am. Seven hours had passed and I had no memory of having slept.

'Jesus Christ, George. I'm turning into a goldfish – I can't remember anything that happened more than three seconds ago.'

Kotov turned uncomfortably in his bag. 'Go back to sleep, you crazy Irishman,' he rasped. With that he pulled, from under his bag, a flask of his cherished Russian vodka and offered me a belt. As he sat up sipping his favourite drink, he lit a cigarette with all the ease of a man at a bar.

'And you think I'm crazy. Are all Russians as mad as you?'

Then from what looked like a pile of old rags in the dim light, Maciej grunted – 'would you two go back to sleep.'

At first light we arose to another bitterly cold morning. The inner surface of the tent above my head was dusted with frozen condensation which would turn to droplets of precipitation once the stove had been fired-up. By 6am we had hastily breakfasted and packed our gear to make a bid for Camp Three above 8,000 metres. The mountain became steeper and the snow deeper and deeper. Conditions were piss-poor that particular morning and neither one of us was at all happy about the 'feel' of the snow. Snow on a mountain can adopt many and varied properties governed by multiple factors like wind speed, temperature, surface gradient and sunshine.

The more you climb on snow, the more accustomed you become to its vagaries. Many experienced climbers believe in an acquired extra-sensory perception of sorts. On occasion I have heard the alarm bells go off in my head warning me to 'get off' a particular section of snow-blanketed mountain, fast.

One hour on the road to Camp Three, wading through deep snow on a steep section where we would have been happier to deal with some icy rock, we had only managed to gain some 350 feet.

Then it happened. For no apparent reason all three of us had an eerie feeling of foreboding. It could have been brought on by sheer exhaustion and oxygen starvation, stuck to a wall of wind-lashed snow and ice at a height where jet planes cruise. But maybe we were picking up some instinctive message. In any case, with the weather showing distinct signs of disimprovement we decided to retreat to Advance Base Camp and fight the mountain another day.

Shortly after our slow and steady drop to Advance Base Camp, which took the full day, the whole of the mountain between 7,538 metres (24,700 feet) and 8,153 metres (26,700 feet) avalanched and destroyed our previous week's work under an incomprehensible and thunderous display of Chomolungma's daunting anger.

Camp Two was obliterated, the tents, sleeping bags and all other gear buried under the massive avalanche of debris.

We were all again assembled at Advance Base Camp feeling frustrated and edgy as time slipped quickly by. The mountain had thrown everything it could at us but we handled the adverse conditions well as a team. In the coming days, however, this co-operative spirit would change utterly.

We had begun to spring-board from Camp One, which was re-stocked with the vital supplies needed for a summit attempt, and to re-establish Camp Two. After considerable effort and long, endless hours of snow-climbing, tents were again pitched at 7,900 metres (25,900 feet). Having created this base more bad luck arrived on the scene travelling at over 100 miles per hour. Scientists call it a tubular high speed current of air near the tropopause or jet-stream wind. It comes out of nowhere and without warning. One moment you are standing at high altitude in still air. The next, you cannot stand on your feet such is the force of the gale which begins with a scary, unannounced suddenness. The tents at Camp Two were ripped from their moorings and swept off the slope like newspapers along a wind-blown city street.

I could see in the tired, gaunt faces of my colleagues the hurt and frustration which was also beginning to painfully gnaw on my resolve. We were really taking a battering but we were not giving up, not yet. For five weeks we struggled to stamp our footprints at Camp Three, some 8,300 metres above sea level.

3 October, 1993 is a day I will not forget easily. The time had come to review the situation. Tough decisions had to be made when it became clear that bad weather conditions and consequent delays would prevent all members of the team summitting. The general consensus was that the first to go for the top would be Maciej and Larkpa and then George or myself with Angbabu, one of our most experienced Sherpas. Jon Tinker, our leader, was to be at Advance Base Camp and, subsequently, the North Col, co-ordinating the attempts on the summit.

Jon decided to monitor the members by two criteria – an ability to carry heavy packs to 7,060 metres (23,000 feet) and to sleep at 7,900 metres (25,900 feet) without oxygen – before the team would decide on the climbers for the summit push.

On 3 October, a team meeting was convened, time was fast running out and we had to select summit teams. Five of the group, including myself and two Sherpas, were picked for the first summit assault. None of us had been unaffected by the harsh and energy-draining conditions of the past weeks. Breathing had become easier as we grew accustomed to the thin air but I remained conscious of the fact that up here, in the domain of the mountain gods, man could not survive indefinitely.

The day before I planned to leave the North Col with Maciej and two Sherpas – George having decided to await a later attempt to stage a summit assault – I noticed a change in Karl's demeanour especially. As he conducted his scientific tests here at Advance Base Camp his movements were slow and ponderous. His face was gaunt and weather-beaten but we all looked as if we needed a bath, shave, square meal, a few pints and a long rest.

On the morning of 4 October, Karl awoke from a fitful sleep, suffering from lack of breath. His chest heaved as if he had just run a marathon. He struggled from his sleeping bag and when standing found he had lost all sense of balance. I accompanied Karl to the mess tent and informed Jon of his condition before I left for the North Col with provisions which would be used on the summit push.

'It's pulmonary oedema, of that I'm certain,' said Tinker, as we debated the best course of action. Thoughts of summitting disappeared completely with the shock of watching a climbing colleague expire before my eyes.

On arrival at the North Col, four hours later, I radioed Advance Base Camp and was told Karl's condition had disimproved rapidly and a full scale rescue would be activated in a bid to get him down the mountain.

A rescue at 6,400 metres (21,000 feet)! I knew, as did everyone else, that such a thing was solely in our hands – no rescue helicopter could even get close to Advance Base Camp. Karl had to be carried over perilously steep tracts of snow and ice. And, somehow, this would have to be done quickly. As the rescue was swung into operation, Karl was placed in a 'Gamow Bag', which is rather like a collapsible de-compression chamber and he was fed with life-giving oxygen. Abandoning my summit attempt I quickly retreated to assist with the evacuation. An ambulance team of eight climbers and Sherpas dropped from Advance Base Camp down the glacier in wind-lashed, less than ideal conditions.

Stopping at intervals, Karl was fed from oxygen bottles but despite this and the time he had spent in the 'Gamow Bag', he showed no signs of recovery. His suffering was a grim and mournful reminder of mountain climbing's dark side.

Hours passed as the team slowly moved down the glacier. Below them stretched a vast expanse of frozen wasteland to Advance Base Camp. Exhausted, the rescue team rested for the night. When I reached them early the following morning another name had been added to the list of men and women who have sacrificed themselves to this mountain.

Karl Heinze, who paid the ultimate price, and his gravestone.

The summit of Everest from the North Col.

At 1am on 5 October, 1993 Karl died with one last, searing heave of his fluid-filled lungs. Tears ran down my face as I stood there looking at his life-less body. I quietly prayed and my mind returned to just days earlier when Karl and I had discussed the impossibility of staging a hasty rescue above 20,000 feet. In hindsight, it was as if he had received some portent of his fate.

In a solemn and surreal ceremony, we buried Karl in the ice of the East Rongbuk glacier after a full, video-taped examination of the body by our team doctor who had arrived from Base Camp as part of the rescue response. Extracts from the Bible were read at that icy tomb on which we placed Karl's NASA cap. I walked dejectedly away leaving a friend and team-mate in the lap of Chomolungma.

The mood, on our return to Advance Base Camp, was understandably sombre. I had encountered death on the mountains before. This was, however, the first time a man with whom I was climbing had perished. On Everest you walk and climb with death, we all knew that. Karl's passing would not discourage us from the task before us.

Four days after the burial, Maciej and Larkpa – having made it through mixed weather to Camp Three, at 8,300 metres – were granted a weather gap through which they climbed the summit ridge to the top of our world. Their achievement rekindled our passion and I eagerly awaited the moment I too would be granted an audience on Chomolungma's high sanctuary.

While Maciej was heading for the top, Jon asked me if he could take my place and go with Angbu to High Camp providing rescue cover for the pair nearing the summit. In the wake of our colleague's death he felt it was his responsibility to oversee the safe return of the summit team.

The following day, 10 October, Jon Tinker, in the company of Sherpa Angbu, achieved his lifetime ambition – the summit of Everest, on his third attempt. Four had now made it to the top but none other would. Jet-stream winds created an invisible and impenetrable barrier as the top of Everest disappeared inside the cloak of a violent tempest.

The expedition was over. Time had run out. As a team effort it had been a success. We had, after all, placed four people at the summit of the highest mountain on earth. And, of course, I felt both elated by this and, at the same time, as frustrated as a shit-house rat not to have the pleasure of placing my country's Tricolour at the top step of this stairway to heaven.

Sure, I felt disappointed but not defeated. Not only had four of the team summitted, but we had also pioneered a variation on the North Ridge route above 8,000 metres which shaved a few hours hours off the climb.

On his return to Advance Base Camp, Jon and I had a lengthy conversation during which he apologised for allowing his summit ambition to override the earlier understanding he had with me and the group.

'It's all right, I understand. When you're up there and the opportunity presents itself how could you not go for it? I'm just pissed-off that I never got the chance. But, I'll be back,' I said and shook his hand firmly.

'Do you mean that, Pat? Do you want another crack at it? This was my third attempt.'

'Try and stop me.'

I liked and understood Jon. We decided, before I left Base Camp, that when his next licence for an Everest permit came through in 1995, if I wanted to return he would leave a place open on the team for me at a cost price not greater than $15,000. This was the only way he felt he could make it up to me. Back at Base Camp I packed my gear for the return home and bade my final farewells to the team, some of whom I would meet on the mountains again.

I had learned much while reaching my personal height record of over 8,000 metres, into the 'Death Zone'. I had witnessed the horrific effects of high-altitude sickness and frostbite. I had witnessed fierce avalanches, the biggest I had ever seen and sat out weeks of harsh weather in tiny tents lashed to the mountain. I had

Yak herders celebrating the team's success on the mountain.

seen how a team representing nine different countries could work together to achieve a common objective. The diverse races camped on the mountain greatly excited me – mountaineers from all over the world. We were all there as citizens of the world attempting the highest peak. Bad weather had provided a lot of tent-bound time discussing a range of issues. I was bursting with interest. I had gone to Everest to climb a mountain and found it had awakened in me a whole area of interest in the cultures of the world and the common traits of all mankind.

On my return home to my family, friends and the beloved hills of Kerry I deliberated deeply on the experience. Long periods of doubt, desires, pain, anguish and elation were gone through before I finally decided to go back. One person in particular was central to my decision – Con Moriarty, my close friend and mentor. Thrashing around Kerry with Con put a lot of things into perspective. I reflected on my life and short climbing career to date of only a few years. I had experienced far greater disappointment in my life before climbing than that of not topping Everest and learned the hard way a lot of lessons on the trials of life.

Using what many might regard as a sort of strange logic, as part of my return match with Everest I would attempt on a bigger project. I knew deep in my heart and soul that I had the other 800 metres in me. A new project evolved, taking into consideration my feeling of wanting to learn more about the cultures and traditions of the people I had met on the expedition. To climb the seven summits became my focus – the highest point on each of the seven continents – to mix culture and adventure. Mount Everest, the highest point in Asia, would only be part of that goal. The plan would dominate the next four years of my life and take me right around the globe to the remotest and highest corners of each continent.

Beside the physical aspects of climbing the mounain there were other sides to the Everest expedition. Karl had told me that while orbiting the earth, during his work as an astronaut with NASA, he felt as if Everest emitted a type of energy which would one day draw him to Chomolungma. In the weeks before his death we spent many long hours chatting and he impressed me greatly with his desire to understand the 'spirit' of places like the Himalaya. Deeply shocked by his death, I now found myself reflecting extensively on my own life.

The First of Seven

Toil and pleasure, in their natures opposite, are yet linked together in a kind of necessary connection.

Livy

'Did you say there's a German stranded on a cliff?'

'No, it's a shepherd,' replied the person at the other end of the telephone. 'German Shepherd. Can you get him off? He's been there for over a week.'

By 1994, I had earned quite a reputation as a mountaineer or, at least, somebody who liked to climb sheer faces. My 'Seven Summits Challenge' was widely covered in the press, a development I hoped would help me to find commercial sponsorship for my expeditions.

'Pat Falvey wants to climb to the top of the highest point on Earth not just because it's there but because it's every mountaineer's ambition to achieve the ultimate.

'This June, the 37 year-old father of two will travel with a nine-strong team to Alaska to take on Mount McKinley – for one of the potentially coldest climbs in his illustrious career on the mountains.

The McKinley expedition will be part of the intensive training for Everest 1995 when Falvey returns to the Himalayan heights with an international team who plan to launch an assault on Everest's notorious north ridge,' began an article in *The Examiner.*

That same newspaper item had prompted an inspector with the Cork Society for the Prevention of Cruelty to Animals (CSPCA) to give me a call. A dog was trapped on a sandstone cliff on the eastern fringe of the city. Nobody knew how it managed to find itself in such a predicament and the CSPCA had failed in their attempts to rescue the distressed animal.

Happy to oblige, I headed off with my climbing gear in the boot of the car. Just off the Lower Glanmire Road a crowd of on-lookers had gathered at the base of the cliff which rises steeply at the rear of a terrace of houses. There I met Mick McCarthy and Don Murphy from SARDA, the Search and Rescue Dogs Association.

112

Peering down from a ledge, about seventy feet up the cliff, was the dog which had obviously scrambled down some twenty feet from the top.

I was lowered to the narrow ledge by Don and Mick and was more than slightly apprehensive about suddenly dropping in on such a large and nervous animal. As I tried to catch him with a noose attached to a long pole, the animal inched his way to the very edge of the shelf on which we stood. The dog had two choices – either fall over the edge or take me on. He savagely growled like a rabid beast, his teeth bared and saliva dripping from his jaw. Now I began to back off, terrified that any second he would attack. With a swift lunge, which was not exactly unanticipated, the dog sprang towards me. As luck would have it he jumped, head first, through the noose enabling me to pin him to the rock face.

Writhing, the deranged animal tried desperately to free himself as I struggled to attach a muzzle and harness. Don Murphy dropped onto the ledge with me and together we managed to 'straight-jacket' the dog. Before an audience of at least 200 on-lookers – many of whom picked up the story live on local radio – I was lowered over the edge with the demented dog clipped on to my harness. He struggled to break loose every inch of the way.

About fifty feet from the bottom, the violently wrestling animal suddenly became still as if to pose for the press photographers on the ground. The shot was captured by *The Examiner* and carried on the front page the following morning. The photograph, showing an alert rather than psychotic german shepherd being held like a lap dog, as we both descended the rope, led to follow-up interest on national radio.

When asked how I managed to calm the dog to enable the photographer to capture the image, I explained that I too had been surprised by the dog's sudden change in temperament. On a nearby rooftop, the canine had spotted a topless sunbather rise from her deck chair to satisfy her curiosity about a man and a dog on the cliff side behind her house.

'So, that's what you were up to,' I said to the dog as I waved to the young lady and descended the cliff face.

Having been picked up as a colour story in the media it provided further leverage with which I could attempt to raise some decent sponsorship. A company called BOC Gases was the first to seize the opportunity and rowed-in behind me providing grant aid for the seven summits project.

And what became of the dog? He was adopted by a local family who christened him 'Kerry' after the Kerry Mountain Rescue Team.

In May, 1987, an Iraqi missile mistakenly hit a American warship in the Persian Gulf and, understandably, the Americans were going berserk.

'Things are hotting up in The Gulf,' said the figure behind the counter raising his eyes from the front page of the morning paper. 'Can I help you with anything?'

I was standing in Con Collins' Bookshop in Cork's city centre.

The shop, a traditional-styled premises in the old Huguenot Quarter just off Patrick Street, is widely known among the climbing and hill walking fraternity as 'the place' for books on those subjects. I casually introduced myself and told Con what I was looking for – guide books and maps of the Alps.

'Going to do some climbing in the Alps? I have been there a number of times myself. When are you off?'

I explained the plan was to go out in about six months time for the next winter season. 'I've never climbed there in winter. The conditions can be quite extreme. Do you not think it could be risky?'

'Not at all,' I responded adopting the 'where ignorance is bliss, 'tis folly to be wise' tack, especially having heard Con tell of his 1982 two-man expedition to the 6,769 metre (22,000 feet) Menthosa peak in Himachal Pradesh in the Himalaya.

Con took a number of books off the shelves and we began to discuss their contents with a shared enthusiasm. An hour later, I left the shop with my purchases under my arm and a distinct feeling that Con and I might one day climb together. On that first encounter, however, he told me he had 'hung up his boots' in order to devote all his time and energy to the shop which he had opened just the previous year.

In the early 1990s, I bumped into Con on the Kerry hills – he was back on the mountains with a renewed passion or, as he put it himself, 'it was either get back into climbing or go mad'. Con expressed a keen interest in my seven summits project – one which would soon take on two dimensions in his capacity both as a climber and publisher. In 1993, Con was still working hard on the establishment of the bookshop as well as a publishing interest but getting out on the mountains every other weekend. That year, he met with Mick Murphy whose ascent of Ama Dablam in 1991 had impressed him greatly.

Murphy was to be the leader of an expedition to North America's highest mountain, McKinley, which, for nearly 100 years, has drawn mountaineers from every corner of the earth. Himalayan veteran Doug Scott referred to McKinley – known to the North American natives as *Denali*, 'The High One' – as equivalent to a 24,000 feet Himalayan peak. The mountain has also been referred to as one of the most dangerous on earth because of the prolonged and savage snow storms which lash the 'High One' throughout the year. The entire Alaskan range, dominated by Denali, is notoriously unforgiving of inexperienced climbers but Murphy was impressed with Collins' curriculum vitae and invited him on board.

The other members of the team included Phil O'Flynn, an experienced trekker; Finbarr Desmond, a technically accomplished climber and at 22 years of age the youngest of the crew; Kate Pollock who had climbed in the Alps a number of times; Barry Keane, an experienced Alpinist and guide book writer; and two Northern Ireland climbers, Clive Roberts and Garth Pearson, who joined the expedition via mutual contacts in Dublin mountaineering circles. This was a well-balanced team of mountaineers with either high-altitude experience or a driving ambition to scale higher peaks.

In May, 1994, the entire team gathered to walk the Maumturk Mountains in Connemara, County Galway, described by Lloyd Praeger in his classic book about rambling throughout Ireland, *The Way That I Went*, as 'a glorious day's walking'. The latter description somewhat belies the fact that this is a nine hour, fifteen-mile slog over some of the toughest terrain. This was to be our last pre-Alaska sortie and it turned out to be a very pleasurable weekend for everyone. Before returning home we visited the Burren in neighbouring County Clare to do some rock-work.

This included filling large plastic drums with heavy stones and dragging them over the rough ground in a bid to determine the best way to hitch on a sled – something we would have to use in order to haul our gear up the first 14,000 feet of snow-covered Denali.

On the morning of 1 June, 1994, we assembled at Cork Airport for the London-Seattle-Anchorage flight, the first leg of my seven summits adventure. There was a great sense of team spirit but I felt an affinity with Collins. This became reinforced when we arrived in Talkeetna, a small frontier outpost of timber-frame shacks with a population of about 300 souls, 120 km from Anchorage.

We were booked into Doug Geeting's bunk-house. Geeting is one of the living legends of backwoods Alaska – a native Californian who runs a small aviation business flying climbers, hunters, anglers, trekkers and general outdoor types into the most inaccessible parts of the magnificent and largely unspoiled land-scape. The bunk-house was packed, stuffy and in a state of on-going construction. The ground floor was littered with building materials and the detritus of those who fled the 'lower 48' United States – canoes, old traps, skis, snow shoes and other bits and pieces.

'Jesus, it's stifling. Open a window,' I said as we unpacked our gear.

'The fuckin' things are jammed.'

'Aw! Fuck this. I'm not staying here. We're going to die in this place. What do you reckon Con?'

'I'm out of here.'

So, Con and I headed off in search of alternative lodgings. We did not have to go far before finding just the place – a beautifully located rustic log cabin on the outskirts of Talkeetna. It stood on the edge of a river, surrounded by lush woodland. I felt as if I had walked on to the set of a Western movie. We did not exactly have this to ourselves as the remainder of the team – who stayed at Geeting's – dropped in regularly to use the shower, kitchen and even sleep in our beds. The decision to rent the cabin, while dent-ing our budget, was based on my credo that, when taking on a big mountain, it is best to, wherever possible, place yourself in an envi-ronment conducive to rest and relaxation.

Over the next few days, as we waited in this wilderness – which over the generations attracted dreamers, hunters, trappers, prospectors, loners and adventurers – we went white water rafting and in search of the area's unique wildlife such as eagles, bears and caribou. Knowing what lay ahead – long days hauling sleds laden with sixty pounds of equipment coupled with back packs contain-ing another twenty to forty pounds up steep, snow-covered and crevasse-blighted mountain – we were determined also to enjoy our creature comforts for as long as we possibly could.

On Sunday, 5 June, one of Doug Geeting's Cessna 185s – which had the capacity to carry either two passengers and gear or four passengers and no gear – carried the team to Base Camp, 7,100 feet up on the Kahiltna Glacier. The flight was extraordinary. Packed in like sardines, the ski-plane lifted us above the tundra. We flew below a ceiling of dense cloud, sweeping over the vast and rugged landscape. The wing tips of the little plane appeared to have mere inches to spare as we followed the meandering ridgelines. This was an awe-inspiring place.

Holding the contours of the ridges, we flew deeper and deeper into the majestic mountain ranges as the cloud cover prevented our escape to a more elevated flight path. Our pilot Doug was part of an elite group of fly-by-the-seat-of-your-pants bush aviators. Massive peaks poked through the cloud ceiling. This was my first time flying in such surroundings, and I was fearful that the craft would be dashed against one of the immense mountain tops by the extreme turbulence we encountered. Tossed about like a toy plane in the hands of a boisterous child, Doug remained calm and composed – he had made this trip more times than he could recall. The plane was drawn towards a huge glacier in the distance. Soon, we could detect red markers on the ice white surface below, our landing strip.

The nose of the Cessna dropped suddenly as did our altitude. We hit the surface with a rebounding thud, bouncing violently along the frozen strip before coming to a welcome halt at Base Camp. We had opted to take the West Buttress route to the summit which was eighteen days climb away, weather permitting. If all went well, we planned to take on the West Rib also. The West Buttress is probably the most popular route on Denali. About three-quarters of the climbers who take to the mountain each year opt for this course. The mountain has a 50% success rate but ferocious weather and McKinley's great height have taken their toll.

The evening before we left Talkeetna, the bush town closed in mourning for two popular Korean climbers who had frozen to death as they climbed an ice route at 15,000 feet. The McKinley guides believed the pair had insufficient provisions and a poor assortment of gear.

That same season, an American climber, Rick Taylor – whom I would later meet on Kilimanjaro – was climbing with his girlfriend when they fell while doing a traverse from 17,000 to 18,000 feet. As they rolled like rag dolls down the steep icy slope the woman lost her hat and he lost his gloves. They came to a halt hundreds of feet from where the accident happened. When rescuers finally came upon them the woman, because of her uncovered head, had frozen to death in the snow. Her partner lost every finger because of frost-bite.

The oddest climbing incident to occur during our stay concerned a Ukrainian solo climber who was found suffering from exhaustion and over-exposure by two Americans halfway up the mountain. When they came upon him he was digging a snow cave in which to sleep, with his hands, like a dog in the sand. On his head he wore a construction worker's hard hat and this was his most elaborate piece of gear. The Americans took him to their tent, wrapped him in a sleeping bag, plied him with hot drinks and orchestrated his rescue. Five days later he was plucked to safety by a parks service helicopter when the winds died down sufficiently to enable the chopper to land safely.

Denali's weather extremes are the stuff of mind-boggling legend. Winds in excess of 100 miles per hour are not uncommon. The temperatures on the mountain have fluctuated between a summer reading of 39 degrees Celsius on Kahiltna to a winter low of minus 70 degrees Celsius. As we flew over Base Camp Con remarked on the circular indentations in the snow where teams had dug-in their tents before moving up the mountain. 'They look just like ancient ring forts, Pat.' At Base Camp we, in turn, dug in our tents to reduce wind resistance in the event of a sudden storm.

The day was cool and clear. The views surrounding us were breathtaking. On every side some of the most beautiful mountains on earth dominated the sky line – Mount Frances, Foraker, Hunter and Crosson all covered in snow and bedecked with immense glaciers. Still 'high' and exhilarated from the excitement of the plane journey into this wonderland of snow and ice and mountain we organised our gear and, like children during winter's first snow-fall, had a great snow-ball battle.

The following morning I rose early in this land of the midnight sun. It was a cold, clear, crisp day. It would be many hours before the sun removed the chill from the air. Before venturing outside, I decided to empty my bladder into my pee bottle.

'What's that noise?' said Collins as his head emerged, tortoise-like, from his sleeping bag. 'For a while there, Falvey, I thought a moose was pissing against the side wall of the tent.'

The first step up McKinley is actually down a hill, Heartbreak Hill, so named because on the return from the mountain, exhausted and hungry, it's a physical and psychological barrier standing in the way of the sanctuary of Base Camp. After breakfast, the team headed down Heartbreak Hill hauling our fibre glass sleds behind us like giant pea pods. In train-like formation we made slow but steady progress across the névé.

The sleds veered with a mind of their own for the first few hours until we mastered the most efficient and safest way to harness them to our bodies. Pulling them was, in the words of Collins, 'fucking brutal', but there was no other way to carry our gear over this increasingly steep and snow-clad terrain which hid crevasses into which a sixteen-wheeled truck could easily be swallowed.

From the onset, Con and I adopted a strategy different to the others. We rose early, sometimes just after midnight, when the 'midnight sun' gave enough light in which to climb. Our reasons for doing this were simple. Before the sun rose high in the sky, the ice under foot was solidly frozen and, consequently, easier to walk on. The rays of the noonday sun bouncing off the reflective ice and snow sapped the energy and burned and weathered any unprotected skin to the consistency of old shoe leather. The difference in the feeling on the skin from noonday sun to midnight shade may be the same as a drop of 14 degrees Celsius.

The remainder of the team tended to rise later after a long night's sleep and cover as much ground as was physically possible each day.

Because of additional camera gear, including solar panels and batteries I had packed to shoot a film of our exploits, Con and I would have to make an extra carry-trip to each camp. After our one mile downhill traipse, we came off the tributary we were on and hit the main Kahiltna glacier. We then turned north to the 7,000 foot contour at the base of the first of many steep rises, a place renowned for its crevasses. Pulling a sled over such ground is sobering stuff. We remained ever mindful of the hopelessness of a situation in which the sled's weight might go crashing through the ground into a hidden fissure in the mountain and drag us helplessly behind it.

Going up hill was a panting, puffing, sweating, swearing task.

'Mush Collins, mush!' or other similar sled-dog instructions usually resulted in a returning barrage of expletive-laden malediction.

After a six hour trek we were both feeling 'shagged' and dehydrated but our thoughts were firmly focused on our first ground level view of McKinley. Here, at Camp One, on a large basin area at 7,700 feet, below Ski Hill, 'The High One' looked awesome against a blue sky backdrop.

Flanked on all sides by peaks lesser in height but no less impressive, Denali stood austere and alluring. The scale and grandeur of this mountain monarch surrounded by its courtiers had a hypnotic effect. The return to Kahiltna base took less than three hours. The sleds had been unloaded and the promise of food, drinks and rest was all the incentive we required to hasten our journey.

We climbed high each day, stashed our gear and slept low. This, we figured, was the best possible way of assisting the body to cope with high altitude and avoid the dreaded acute mountain sickness. One climber we encountered from Colorado, who lived in a town at 8,000 feet above sea level, started spitting up blood when he reached 10,000 feet. This was a striking illustration of the 'who's it going to be next?' uncertainty of thin-air disorders.

From our camp at 11,000 feet the going got tougher and we all started to feel the breathlessness and occasional headaches and nausea caused by the altitude. Otherwise, everything went smoothly. We continued to establish new camps and then drop back to the previous one to rest up and replenish our dehydrated bodies.

En route to each camp, we encountered many climbers of many nationalities. The popularity of this mountain, especially among North Americans, creates its own problems. In 1992, a team of volunteers led by parks service personnel spent an entire day at 17,200 feet digging up the frozen excrement left by climbing teams and dumping the waste into nearby crevasses. Trash and abandoned food and fuel caches frequently litter the slopes and, unfortunately, not even the winter storms cover all of what one Denali ranger described as 'these insults to the mountain'.

At 14,300 feet, we were forced to abandon our sleds. No tears were shed. There were times when I felt like I was pulling a tour bus behind me and with that thought my mind raced back to Kathmandu and the Ama Dablam expedition in 1991.

'Hey! Con. Did I ever tell you about Dick Baba?'

'Only about fifty times, Pat.'

'Is that all? Jaysus, you probably have the story forgotten so.'

The final stage to our camp at 14,300 feet was sheer punishment – a long slope which made my back-pack feel as if it was gaining weight with every cramponed step I took.

We pitched our tents on an ice bowl. At this stage Con and I were a day ahead of the rest of the group and we decided to go to 16,000 feet to acclimatise. On our return, the others were assembled at the ice bowl. We agreed it was best to rest for a few days before going any further. At 3pm that day, a ranger who is stationed throughout the climbing season in a pre-fabricated hut, informed us that there was a major storm heading our way in the next forty-eight hours. The bad weather could last for several days or several weeks, he casually stated. It was decision time – 'do we stay or do we go for the top in advance of the snowstorm?' An emergency team meeting was held.

Murphy, Desmond, Collins and I were the only ones in the team who felt fit enough to race to the summit 6,000 feet above us before the storm system moved in. As we prepared in silence for our drive to the top, an over-heard conversation between two Americans camped nearby brought smiles to our faces.

One asked the other if he thought the Irish climbers they had seen drinking beer at Chilkoot Charley's pub in Anchorage were still there knocking them back. These two lads, who were oblivious to our presence at 14,300 feet, failed in their summit attempt. Maybe they should have stayed at Chilkoot Charley's!

Glasnost was in the air and camped here also were a team of Russians dressed in jeans and trainers – steel hard people whom, we presumed, would not attempt the summit in such casual dress.

The 'fab four' left this camp at 9pm on 13 June, ten days into the expedition. The sky was filled with the majestically filtered light of the low-lying sun. Our intention was to push the 6,000 feet to the summit in one push before the storm would cut us off.

Our first bus stop to the top was the Crow's Nest at 17,200 feet along the final stages of the West Buttress where we encountered some of the steepest, most exposed climbing. We made good, incident-free progress with Collins and myself working as a team. But this was no place for a Sunday stroll.

A thunderous clap from behind froze us in our tracks. Far

121

The summit party on Denali with, left to right, Con Collins, Pat Falvey, Mick Murphy and Finbar Desmond.

below us on the buttress a few acres of snow had slipped off the ridge and avalanched over the almost vertical western side. Through our glasses we could see two climbers standing just feet from the shear-off point of the avalanche – they must have been terrified.

Later as we walked along the ridge leading to the 'Nest, the sky was illuminated with the pink-orange hue of the midnight sun reflected on exposed sections of the mountain's granite carapace. It was decided to stop at 17,200 feet for a break and stash some provisions for the return journey in a snow cave. The tent was pitched and we began melting snow to provide the drinks we needed to rehydrate our systems.

The tent which we had pitched could provide crucial sanctuary on our return journey if there was a sudden break in the weather. We shared the task of melting the snow and ice, in relay. While three rested in the tent, the other boiled the water.

We evacuated the tent shortly before 6am. From the Crow's

Nest the route followed a rising traverse to the 18,200 feet Denali Pass. A fall here would send you rocketing to the glaciers below. We carried little and debated whether or not we should pack a rope. We decided to make do with fifteen metres of walking rope, despite Con's hesitation.

Progress was punishingly slow along the traverse to the 'Pass and Con complained that his feet were freezing. 'If we don't move faster, I'll get frostbite. My toes are freezing,' Con moaned.

Finbarr was feeling unwell and at the 'Pass we decided to pair off. Mike and Finbarr would rest here and Con and I would press ahead.

As we climbed we discussed Finbarr's condition and both of us agreed he was showing signs of acute mountain sickness with the toughest part of the climb still before him. We struggled on. There was no turning him back. Finbarr was determined to spend his birthday atop Denali.

Conditions were freezing on the ridge. Our toes and fingers constantly reminded us of the below zero temperature. However, from here, we could see storm clouds gathering on the horizon. It was vital to get to the top as quickly as possible and the weight you carry is directly proportional to the progress you make. Looking east I thought 'thank God we're almost there'. But, almost there was a place called the Archdeacon's Tower, a false summit.

At 19,600 feet, feeling cold, hungry and gasping for air and liquid, we crossed the ludicrously christened Football Field – a broad and exposed plateau – and there 700 feet above us was the crown of the 'High One'. Climbing the first 400 feet on the headwall was cruel. Tired, thirsty and as exposed and ill at ease as a bishop in a brothel, we struggled on praying that the approaching storm was not in any great hurry. At this point bad weather would have had fatal consequences. Had Mick and Finbarr retreated? We did not know.

The final 300 feet were along a spectacular summit ridge leading to the small, well-defined top. We summited at 2.45pm on Tuesday, 14 June after eighteen hours arduous climbing from the ice bowl camp site. With tears in our eyes we hugged each other and offered mutual congratulations.

'One down, six to go Pat,' said Con, as he took photographs from the highest ground on North America. 'Come on, let's get off this ridge,' knowing that, despite fatigue, we would have to drop to the Crow's Nest where our tent stood waiting.

Taking a last few moments to record the views in our minds and savour the taste of triumph, we then took the first steps on the arduous return journey while to the north a dark lowering cloud mass headed our way.

An hour later we met Mick and Finbarr just below the summit ridge. Finbarr was lying on the snow in a troubled and exhausted state. 'We're going to rest for an hour here and then make for the summit,' Mick said, matter of factly.

At 5.25pm we arrived back at our tent on the 'Nest. Feeling drained of all energy, even getting the stove started was a burdensome task. Two hours later the snow began to fall from a sky which veiled the light. There was still no sign of Mick and Finbarr. A further two hours passed by which time Con and I were deeply concerned as we felt they should have arrived before now. Having rested and rehydrated we geared-up and went off in search of the two lads fearing the worst. Not long after leaving our tent we encountered a few climbers on their way back from the summit. They informed us that they had met Finbarr and Mick who, they assured us, were safe and on their return journey down to us.

Shortly before midnight, three figures walked slowly towards our tent. Mick and Finbarr had made it to the summit. Finbarr, suffering from acute mountain sickness, collapsed at the pinnacle and had no recollection of ever having beeen there. They were accompanied by a Swiss doctor who, with other Denali climbers, aided

Our tent dug in at 14,200 feet on Denali (McKinley).

Finbarr's tortuous trek from the top.

We spent that night in the small tent. Nobody slept well. The following day we broke camp and headed off early with Finbarr in a very frail and disimproved condition. He needed constant watching on the drop to 14,200 feet. On arrival there we discovered Garth had had enough and was gone home. Barry plied us with hot drinks. That evening the storm unleashed its full arsenal. It was a total white-out. Looking out the door flap was like staring at a huge sheet of white paper held close to your face. There was not a single feature to be seen, anywhere.

My thoughts ran over the happenings of the past number of days – Finbarr had been fortunate to escape, relatively unscathed. High altitude climbing is a discipline and maybe even an art. It is not only about enduring many types of hardship and diverse weather – most importantly it is about having the ability to read your own body and listen to what it is telling you. If the brain shuts down this line of communication your life can be placed in serious danger from the effects of high-altitude mountain sickness or, worst still, pulmonary or cerebral oedema.

For the next eight days we remained trapped, snowed-in with a motley crew of neighbouring teams. Conditions were too dangerous to allow us move up or down from the position we now involuntarily held. Each day was started with shovel work as we cleared the deep snow from the tents. This had to be done a number of times each day or the huge pressure of accumulating snow would have flattened our camp.

Most evenings were spent in a communal teepee where the *craic*, while being mighty, belied the threat facing us all – famine. Our meagre food supplies were fast running out. If the storm did not abate soon, we would have to either sit and starve or attempt a descent to Base Camp.

On 21 June, the eighteenth day of our expedition, we held a Midsummer Solstice party in the teepee. There was no booze or buffet but we had great fun singing songs and dancing. Here we were, thirty stranded adventurers whose ages ranged from 14 to 73 years, the latter being living proof that old age should never hinder high ambition. We had decided, before the party, that 23 June would mark our departure, no matter what the weather was like. Our food was gone at this camp and nobody had spare provisions.

It was a dread-filled decision but on the morning of our scheduled departure we arose early, dug out the tents from under the night's snow-fall and made ready our evacuation to Base Camp. The outside ground level had risen five feet from the time we arrived here such was the effect of the blizzard. I was to lead the drop to Base Camp with Con, Barry, Finbarr and Kate. We walked all day and into the night. The storm had lost some of its clout and, while the going was energy sapping through deep, fresh snow, at least, for most of the time, we could see clearly where we were headed.

At 4.15am on 23 June we stumbled into Base Camp, exhausted, famished but glad to be off the mountain. Northern climber Clive Roberts and Phil O'Flynn decided to stay on and led by Mick Murphy make an attempt on the summit as soon as conditions were favourable. They would eventually make it to 16,200 feet before a second storm forced them to flee.

That day one of Geeting's daring aviators found a break in the storm clouds and dropped his small ski-plane into Base Camp. Leaving our gear at Base Camp we flew back to Talkeetna, rented a cabin and had our first shower in twenty days. Our flight had been the last for days to come. While waiting to be reunited with our gear, we spent most of our waking hours in the cafés, bars and restaurants of Talkeetna.

Alaska has a tough, last frontier reputation – a place where the winters are bleak and cold, the summers mosquito-ridden and many of the natives oddballs. Men outnumber women by a huge margin which is said to be at its greatest in the McKinley area.

Once off the mountain we went to a local Talkeetna hostelry, the Fairview Inn, to celebrate the success of our expedition. Once inside it was obvious that here was a dearth of women. On this particular night there was one single female in a group of about eighty drinkers. She stood at the bar and as I called a round of drinks I turned to her and chatted politely.

'How's it goin'? Where are you from?' I asked.

'New York, but I've lived here for over five years.'

Before the conversation could proceed further, I felt something vice-like gripping me by the shoulders. I was lifted off the ground. With my legs dangling, I turned to face a big, hairy, bear-headed man who was obviously riled for reasons unknown to me, then.

'Hey! You leave my woman alone,' he said with a bass grunt and dropped me to the floor.

I feebly looked up at this towering and unhappy giant and explained that where I came from it was considered mannerly to converse with all those you encounter at a bar. He thawed out a bit when he discovered I was Irish and told me one of his trapper mates was an Irishman. I stood listening to his banter, too nervous to walk away as the beers I had ordered sat on the counter top.

The others grew impatient and increasingly thirsty. Eventually, Con left his seat and arrived at the bar counter to collect the pitchers of beer. Con crept in behind me, grabbed a few beers and turning to walk away, engaged in conversation with the lady from New York. When the big brute spotted this he caught me by the lapels and hoisted me once more into the air, drawing me level to his beast-like face.

'You tell your fuckin' friend to leave my woman alone,' and with that he dropped me again.

Con quickly scurried back to the table when he saw exactly what had detained me.

Standing in the shadow of this incredibly ugly hulk, lines from the Robert Service poem about 'The Shooting of Dan McGrew' ran through my head –

There's men that somehow just grip your eyes,
and hold them hard like a spell;
And such was he, and he looked to me like a
man who had lived in hell;
With a face most hair, and the dreary stare
of a dog whose day is done ...

Returning to my table and friends, I recounted what had happened at the bar.

'It's true what they say – if you're a woman looking for a man, go to Alaska, ladies, where the odds are good, but the goods are odd.'

Later that night, Con and I became as friendly as we could with the trapper with attitude who invited us to go hunting with him the following day. We refused, of course, not wishing to meet the same fate as the Bold Dan McGrew.

Another evening, we again retired to the local drinking hole. While sinking frothy beers at the bar, the double doors swung open in true wild west fashion and in walked what looked like a cross between a lumberjack and a grizzly bear. He walked to the bar and checked-in a rifle, a holstered side-arm and a large hunting knife which he took from his boot. He then commenced to drink at a rapid rate. He spoke little but was not threatening or unfriendly and joined our party.

Early the following morning, when we had all consumed more beer than was perhaps prudent, the big frontiersman – who told us he tried to get to Talkeetna for a few drinks and buy provisions every six months or so – collected his weapons from the barman.

We left the pub together and said our farewells. I watched him walk down the street and climb into a light plane which looked as if it had been cobbled together with bits of old galvanized iron sheeting. With a burst of black smoke from the exhaust, the plane rattled along the street gathering the momentum needed to carry it into the early morning ether.

Alaska – where the goods are odd!

Before going home Con and I decided to do some sight-seeing which included a short cruise in the Prince William Sound. Here can be seen a staggering array of marine wildlife but the fragility of this unique ecosystem was graphically illustrated on 24 March, 1989 when the giant tanker *Exxon Valdez* ran aground and spilled some 11,000,000 gallons of its 60,000,000 gallon cargo.

This was one of the worst incidents of its kind in modern history and the long-term environmental consequences are still being felt. On the surface, literally, there is little evidence of the widespread and dire damage caused by the oil pollution but under the water's surface the picture is far bleaker. It will take very many years before the marine flora and fauna of the huge area affected by the spill returns to normal or, as close to it as possible in this man-scarred environment.

The *Exxon Valdez* disaster could have been avoided if the US government had listened to the protests of environmentalists at the construction, in 1973, of an oil pipeline from the North Alaskan oilfields to the ice-free port of Valdez. These objectors, regarded as radical 'greenies' at the time, spoke in favour of using the alternative overland pipeline route through Canada to West Coast refineries. Had the views of these environmentalists been taken on board, Alaska would have avoided one of the costliest oil spillages of all time which caused irreparable damage to commercial fishing grounds and marine life across 100 square miles of ocean.

On my travels, I have encountered many different cultures and peoples. Clockwise from top left: Dani, Aborigine, Chinese, Russian, Tibetan and Nepalese.

Top: practising evacuation by cableway during rescue training;
Bottom left: Con Moriarty training in the Gap of Dunloe prior to Ama Dablam; Bottom
right: climbing on Howling Ridge, a classic route on Corrán Tuathail.

Main Photo: ice climbing in Cogne, northern Italy, 1991, during an international meet with Eddie Cooper and Pat Littlejohn. Top inset, retreating on the icefall and, bottom inset, climbing the icefall pillar.

Clockwise from top left: Ama Dablam in the Nepal Himalaya; Corrán Tuathail in Ireland's Macgillycuddy's Reeks, during winter; Kilimanjaro in Tanzania; and Aconcagua in Argentina.

Clockwise from top left: the final 100 metres below the summit of McKinley with, inset, Con Collins on the summit; Con Collins on the ridge above Rescue Gully on McKinley; approaching Camp Two on Ama Dablam; and climbing on the South Ridge of the Eiger.

Top: Ciaran Corrigan suffering from pulmonary oedema and team members concerned for his health; Bottom left: Mick Murphy and his frostbitten toe; Bottom right: James Allen suffered frostbitten fingers.

Clockwise from top: the upper reaches of Everest, fourteen miles from Base Camp at 17,000 feet; Camp One at the North Col; approaching the Third Step on the Ridge; and the avalanche-prone approach to the North Col.

African scenes, clockwise from top left: Massai; Chagga children; zebra; my son Brian and I on top of Kilimanjaro; Joe O'Leary with an African family; and a hippo in Ngorongoro.

Top: Con Collins making his way through the penitentes below Camp One on Aconcagua and bottom: Christmas Day at Camp One on Aconcagua, feeling a little homesick.

Top: a heavily-laden lorry heading for Everest Base Camp; Bottom left: the home of the exiled Dalai Lama in Lhasa, Tibet; Bottom right: Tibetan children play with a balloon in Lhasa.

*Top: Jeff Shea and myself on the summit of Mount Vinson and bottom, the Hercules
plane on the ice runway at Patriot Hills.*

Top: Dani warriors in Irian Jaya; Bottom left: Gene Tangney crossing a reed bridge in the rain forests of Irian Jaya; Bottom right: Dani women lose a finger top when a husband or son dies.

Camp Two on top of the Yellow Tower, Ama Dablam. Inset, approaching Camp Two on the exposed south-west ridge.

Top: storm-bound on McKinley. Every few hours we had to dig our tent out. Inset, Con Collins emerging for a dig; Bottom left: sled-hauling on McKinley; Bottom right: George Kotov on the summit of Elbrus, with Ushba in the background.

Top, guiding on Corrán Tuathail in winter. Left to right, Pat Falvey, Therese Culligan, Frank Greally, Joe Leary and Barry Duncan. Bottom, Pat and family at a reception hosted by Cork Corporation on his return from summitting on Everest.

Pat Falvey on the summit of Mount Everest.

Back home, six months later in what had been a hectic year, I managed to secure a place on an international team heading to Everest in 1995. I also snatched the opportunity to go to Africa with Joe O'Leary and climb Kilimanjaro, the highest free-standing mountain in the world.

THE DARK CONTINENT

The great powers have been to the moon and back. In Africa, however, the village is receding with worsening communications even further into the distance.

Julius Nyerere, President of Tanzania

Feelings of jet lag were well overcome by growing excitement as we approached Kilimanjaro International Airport having hop-scotched across east Africa. Joe and I had gone for the cheapest air package which, like a country bus, stopped at every port en route from London to the Tanzanian safari capital, Arusha.

In the course of the seemingly endless flight we stopped-over in places whose names had a familiar ring but about which we knew very little. Asmara in Eritrea, Addis Abba in Ethiopia, Entebbe in Uganda – these place names conjured up thoughts of adventure and the exotic but such romantic ideas were literally brought down to earth with each landing – every airport terminal had a drab sameness about it and the hours spent waiting for the next leg of the journey to begin were monotonous.

'Here at last Joe! If we had stayed in the air any longer we would have sprouted wings.'

Disembarking from the jet the first thing to strike us was a wall of hot and humid air. The temperature here on our arrival was a far from Irish 39 degrees Celsius. Our sweat pores opened wide to the African heat. By the time we made it to the baggage carousel our shirts were clinging to our wet backs as sweat poured down our faces and chests, and rivulets of perspiration coursed down the cracks of our arses. To any native African it must have looked as if Joe and myself were slowly melting like sculpted lumps of ice taken from a deep freeze and placed in this oven-hot environment.

Laden-down like pack mules, we walked through the main exit of the airport and were halted in our tracks by the glorious sight of our first African sunset. There, to the west, an immense deep orange sun was slowly sinking over the African plains. The colours in the sky, every conceivable variation of red and orange, ran into each other like some boundless abstract watercolour – the art of the

Gods.

We were greeted outside the airport by a tall, black man holding a card aloft with the names 'FAL-V' and 'OH-LEERY'.

'Is that us?' said Joe as his face broke into a huge grin.

'It's you for sure, I always thought you looked a bit leery,' I quipped.

On approaching him I asked if his name was Peter. I had spoken to this man by telephone on numerous occasions having been told of his expertise as an expedition organiser.

'Hello Mr Pat and Mr Joe. Welcome to Tanzania.'

Keeping up a constant barrage of chatter, he escorted us to a waiting jeep. In the first few minutes of our encounter he

Joe O'Leary, one of my best friends, and a partner in Africa.

told us about his childhood, family and business. He was so friendly and unassuming, it was as if we had been re-united with a long-lost cousin.

'Tell me, did you ever kiss the Blarney Stone?' Joe jokingly asked him.

'No. But I would much like to kiss Sharon Stone,' he quickly riposted.

Trundling along the road to Arusha, the ancient, open-topped Land Rover stirred-up a cumulus of dust in its noisy wake. As a sense of Africa unfolded on both sides of the road, Joe's face took on the expression of a shell-shocked soldier. Along the roadside was a constant stream of pedestrians, all ages, some in national dress, others wearing dusty, western clothes. Shanty huts, made from mud blocks and corrugated tin were the dwellings of those who lived in the sprawling Arusha suburbs. There were people everywhere, sitting outside their tiny homes, standing in groups and milling about. The African experience had begun.

In the warm, hazy Tanzanian evening, Joe O'Leary and I were sitting pool-side at our hotel in Arusha. We were familiarising ourselves with a new video camera. Three young, black women walked towards us. They were well dressed, tall, lean and strikingly beautiful. Their oiled hair looked as if it had been sculpted from polished lignite and the sun glistened on the unblemished ebony skin of their faces, arms and legs. Any one of them could have graced a European fashion catwalk with aplomb.

With flashing smiles, they stood before us, introduced themselves in perfect English and asked us if we were the gentlemen they had arranged to meet at this hotel. When it became clear we were not, they apologised and walked back towards the hotel foyer.

In the foyer of the hotel we met a gin-drinking Englishman. When we got talking, he gave me some advice.

'Pat, when you're out in the jungle, there will be great danger from lions. You will be out of your jeep at times. If one of the pride should venture to attack you, wait until it is about to launch itself at you, bend down, pick up a bit of shit and throw it straight between the lion's eyes,' he said, in a serious tone.

I had to ask the obvious question, about how I could be sure that there would be 'ammunition'.

'Don't worry Pat. There'll be shit there. There will be shit there,' he replied as he knocked back his gin.

Later that night, two of the three women we had met earlier walked into the hotel bar where we were having a drink prior to attending a New Year's Eve party. We invited them to join us at our table. They were both in their early twenties and attending university in Kenya. They had replied to a newspaper advertisement seeking young, attractive women to take part in a film. The advertisement had been vague for a reason. A telephone call later and they were here in the hotel to meet the film-maker. He turned out to be a Belgian who was in the porn film business. One of the three, too desperate for whatever little she could earn to fund her time in university, succumbed to this new form of slavery affecting many poor Africans.

'We will do anything to get out of Africa. There is no future here for us – even when we finish our studies,' one of the women declared.

It was not uncommon, they told us, for well-educated women

like them to turn to prostitution, or pornography, to earn enough for survival. During our brief stay in East Africa, we would see many examples of the predatory exploitation of the indigenous people by wealthy, insolent men and women. This was not my first time experiencing the desperation of many people in so-called Third World countries. But in Joe's expression I could see the depth of shock I had experienced on my first visit to Kathmandu.

Peter had invited Joe and I to a party in Arusha. This had been a very long day for us but we were high on adrenalin, stimulated by the sights and sounds of this evocative place. There were about 600 native Africans ringing in the New Year and we were the only whites in the crowd. We spent our time there with Peter (who was to organise the logistics of our African stay) his family and friends. The strains of traditional African music filled the air as a sea of colourfully-dressed revellers danced and mingled in a fug of cigarette smoke and body heat.

Joe and I, who stood out like nudists in a nunnery, caught the amorous attention of two large African ladies dressed in multi-coloured, body-hugging, wrap-around, sarong-type evening dresses. The over-stretched fabric barely managed to contain their bulbous and heaving breasts which in the course of their energetic dance trembled and quivered like baby pigs trying to break out of a poke. They dragged us into the centre of the dancing scrummage where a space cleared and we became the focal point of smiling and joking commentators who regarded us with the same intriguing interest we had for them.

Our first day in Africa was guaranteed to be one neither of us would ever forget – nor were we ever again likely to ring in the New Year in such exotic and agreeable company.

The next morning Peter drew-up in an open truck outside our hotel to take us to the Kibo hotel, about three hours drive away. En route, he stopped at his brother's house to collect his wife, his six children, his sister-in-law and her children. I don't know how we all fitted into the four wheel drive truck but we did, as well as all our gear. Along the road, Peter and his family sang traditional African songs and Joe and I did our best to inject a flavour of our own Irish musical tradition. It was great *craic*.

That night we were introduced to our guide for the Kilimanjaro climb. Whether you join an organised climb or plan your own trek to the top, it is bound by local laws that porters and guides are employed. This is enforced regardless of your skill and experience as a climber.

At the park entrance the following day, we paid our entry fees, hut fees, rescue fees and guide fees. All told, this did not amount to much. A five-day climb along the much-travelled Marangu Route – sometimes referred to as the Coca Cola Route due to its popularity – should not cost the earth. The Park headquarters was bedecked with posters and signs warning visitors of the hazards of mountain sickness and pulmonary oedema.

The trek to the top of the highest free-standing mountain on earth could not be described as a 'Granny Walk', although it is true that many grandmothers have climbed it.

A sacred beacon of many spiritual traditions is the snow-capped volcano which rises high above the east African savannah. The first written record of the majestic mountain appeared in Chinese script in 500 AD when oriental traders led their caravans through its shadow. The Chagga call it 'Kibo' – a word which is thought to refer to the 'white stuff' covering its lofty summit. Snow so near the equator was thought to have been a meteorological impossibility until the exploration of the mountain by westerners in the nineteenth century. Learned geographers, scientists and explorers claimed the white cap was a massive quartz deposit. Even twelve years after its 'western' discovery in 1848 by Johann Ludwig Krapf, a doctor of divinity from Tubingen in Germany, European geographers still refused to accept the mountain as snow-capped. Krapf and his Swiss missionary colleague, Johann Rebmann became the first westerners to leave their footprints on the lower reaches of the mountain during their travels through Africa converting Krapf's 'innumerable heathens'. However, these two never made it to the summit. That prize was grasped by another German, Hans Meyer, who reached the top of Uhuru peak in October, 1889.

The mountain has featured prominently in legend, folklore, history and literature. In *The Snows of Kilimanjaro*, Ernest Hemingway immortalised the discovery near the summit of a frozen leopard in the 1920s. Why this beast had chosen to climb well above its natural habitat has never been fully explained. Today, all that remains of this strange phenomenon is a place on the upper reaches of the mountain called Leopard Point. The petrified carcase of the big cat has long since disappeared.

The mountain can be climbed at any time of the year but the region can be subjected to very heavy rainfall during the months of April, May and November. Climbers with a desire for peace, quiet and solitude on the mountains should bear in mind that Kilimanjaro is one of the biggest tourist attractions on the African continent and the number of expeditioners is growing each year.

We drove a little beyond the entrance gates and before long were on the trail, in shorts and T-Shirt, making our way through tangled rain forest. Most of our gear was carried by porters who had travelled this well-worn path many times.

I felt like a tiny bug walking through a green, deep-pile soggy carpet. Rain beat down on us constantly and there was no wildlife to be seen on the verges of this busy path. For almost seven hours, we walked through the forest. Vines and creepers filled the gaps between the trees, creating verdant walls on both sides of the winding trail. Eventually we came into a clearing where a cluster of huts had been planted by the Park developers. Here, at Mandara Hut, we would spend our first night in the company of many other Kilimanjaro trippers.

A meal of battered fish was prepared for us. It did not taste fresh but I ate it without any gastro-kickback. Joe declined and resorted to his stash of dehydrated concentrates.

'Is there anything you can't eat?' he asked incredulously as I wolfed down Joe's helping of fish.

Day Two found us trekking through the final, upper reaches of the rain forest to 3,000 metres (9,800 feet). At this height we emerged from the moist, humid undergrowth into a belt of alpine meadow. A profusion of wild flowers poked their beauteous heads above the wild grasses. The sky was clearer and the rains remained in our wake.

In the distance, our objective came into view. Kilimanjaro is one of the greatest natural monuments on this earth and one which supports virtually every terrestrial environment – savannah and tropical jungle; alpine meadows and moorland; desert; snowfield and glacier. Just shy of the 4,000 metre (13,100 feet) mark, we halted at Horombo Hut, another cluster of pre-fabricated sleeping shelters with a communal mess building.

'Not battered fish again – are they trying to cod us?' Joe quipped, as I tucked into my double helping.

After dinner, we were sitting and chatting with other Horombo

Hut residents when a party arrived having summitted a day earlier. Among those returning from the top was a young American climber, Rick Taylor, whom I had met on McKinley in 1994. We shook hands and feeling his fingerless grip I was immediately reminded of the tragedy which had altered this young man's life. Rick was also intending to achieve the seven summits goal but, for him, it was a pilgrimage in memory of his late girlfriend. It had been his girlfriend's ambition to climb the seven summits, not Rick's. After her death, he pledged to achieve the dream in memory of her.

On 3 January, we rose with the dawn, said our goodbyes to Rick and the other travellers and headed onwards and upwards, mostly through an arid, dry and vegetation-less landscape which started as abruptly as the moorland had ended. For long hours, we trudged across this boulder-strewn belt of glacial gravel and pumice, lunar-like rocks.

Here, above the 4,000 metre contour, our progress slowed considerably as our lungs worked overtime to extract sufficient quan-

Rick Taylor, who lost eight fingers on Denali from frostbite, and, inset, his damged hands.

tities of oxygen from the rarefied air. Joe complained of headaches but nothing too debilitating. It was his first time ever climbing at high altitude and his determination to reach the summit cast aside all feelings of discomfort.

That evening, we camped at Kibo Hut, 5,000 metres (16,400 feet), had a meal and retired to our beds at 6pm. We slept little at this height. It was also remarkably cold.

We started off on the final leg of the journey just after midnight, dressed in fleeces, down jackets and pants, mindful of the fact our guide had told us we would not need such insulated clothing.

Our head torches lit the way across the final summit zone. The beams of the lamps were reflected by snow and ice. It was biting cold – the air temperature was at least minus 10 degrees Celsius – and I thought of the nineteenth-century 'Doubting Thomases' who decried the first reports that snow was capping a mountain close to the equator.

Moving along the scree towards the crater slope, I let Joe set the pace. It was a privilege for me to climb one of my seven goals in the company of a man who had been one of the mainstays of my global challenge. Joe would probably want to climb higher mountains some day but now this was his 'Everest'.

Approaching the false summit of Gilman's Point across icy scree, the gradient was gentle but, at this height, climbing took great effort. We had earlier encountered a group who retreated from the mountain because of the severe cold and were glad we had packed our down clothing despite the best expert advice to the contrary. Gasping for breath and feeling light-headed, Joe stopped, turned to me and said – 'anyone who does this for fun must be fucking crazy.'

At Gilman's Point, which is 215 metres (700 feet) below Uhuru Peak, our guide turned to us and, with an uneasy smile, said 'this is it, the top'.

We had done our homework and knew too well that this was a stunt often pulled on unsuspecting expeditioners. If a guide can get a party off the mountain without having to go all the way to the top, he will. The *raison d'etre* of each guide is to lead as many parties up the mountain as possible. He gets the same financial reward for those that turn back without ever reaching the summit and if the expedition can be shortened by a few hours, well, this too is a bonus. The guide presented no objection when we told him firmly that our objective was Uhuru which lay at the end of a slowly, rising ridge flanking the summit crater.

The mountain began to grow about 750,000 years ago when volcanic lava spewed from three main points – Shira, Kibo and Mawenzi. Kibo was the last lava flow to remain active and is thought to have become silent about 360,000 years ago. One last pyrotechnical display created the extraordinary caldera just below the summit – an almost perfectly circular crater two-and-a-half kilometres across. Inside this, almost slap-bang in the centre, an inner cone rises to a height which is about 100 metres higher than Gilman's Point and another 100 metres below the summit. Within this cone, there is an inner crater with another cone and in the centre of that a minor cone.

The whole scene gives the impression that when the mountain was a seething, hot mass of lava a massive stone was dropped in its centre and the concentric waves just froze into rock waves.

As we moved along the ridge heading for the top, I could sense Joe's renewed enthusiasm. Pumped with adrenalin, his energy and spirits rose with the sun. The new morning light illuminated an African tapestry of red, orange and gold hues. Neither of us had ever witnessed such an awe-inspiring sunrise. As we climbed ever higher, a rich blue began to slowly fill the sky above. Below us, a motionless plane of cloud shielded much of the African savannah views.

The Rehab group on the summit of Kilimanjaro.

Before us lay one more hour of gentle climbing across this strange and evocative place. Joe shrugged off his earlier sluggishness and focused his attention on the object of our ambition. The low morning light cast an eeriness over the caldera. The inner crater looked like some fantastical island in a sea of ice and snow.

At 10am on 4 January, 1995, we made it to the top of Africa. There was much congratulatory hugging and back-slapping, unaware as we were that the following year we would both return to Kilimanjaro. Despite our jubilation on reaching the top, I knew the summit was not the end of the expedition. Our tired and weary bodies had to be motivated and psychologically re-energised and taken back down the mountain.

Our expedition had taken us from equatorial to arctic conditions all within 74 hours. In tropical 35 degrees Celsius conditions, we had pushed our way through the rain forest up to the alpine meadows, across a lunar-like high desert landscape before reaching the minus 10 degrees Celsius summit of the highest mountain on the African continent. Now it was time to go back the way we had come but we were not heading for home quite yet.

We hired a jeep on our return to Arusha and the services of a Masai cook, Simba and a Chagga driver, John. Simba, 'The Lion' had earned his name because his father had killed a male lion armed only with a short spear. Simba's father had earned the Masai right to wear a traditional lion-mane head-dress of a warrior elite. He had taken the brunt of a lion's charge and had delivered a fatal trust with his spear as part of his initiation into manhood. These days lion hunting is banned but the son of Simba was proud not to have killed a lion but to inherit the name of a lion-killer. Our Chagga driver we had met in Marangu and immediately warmed to his friendliness and infectious sense of humour. John had spent most of his life in and around the foothills of Kilimanjaro as well as having an in-depth and local knowledge of Arusha. This duo knew of our desire to see the 'real' Africa and not just the air-brushed tourist haunts.

Joe, being a secondary school teacher, was keen to visit one of the local schools. To get there we journeyed through the slums of this otherwise attractive town nestled at the foot of Mount Meru. There were children everywhere. Their smiles cast brightness on the dreariness of their impoverished conditions. The adults were indifferent and must have thought – 'they have been on safari, are staying in a plush hotel, and now they want to see how the other half lives.' It is not uncommon for tourists to visit the slums. Were we any better? Were we voyeurs also? Or could we precipitate change by creating an awareness in our own country of the plight of our African brothers and sisters?

Arusha National School was a corrugated iron-clad building with dirt floors and a surface drain leading from hole-in-the-ground toilets to an open sewer in the street. Fifteen hundred children attended class each day, sat on long wooden benches and, with an insatiable appetite for knowledge, hoped education would provide their ticket to a better life – an albeit alien life they had seen on American television shows and films.

Outside the town we were taken to a stone quarry. Here, whole families toiled together – grandparents, parents and their children. Three generations eking out a living. The men pounded the rocks with coarse steel hammers and chisels. The women and children gathered the tiny pieces and created a mound of rock fragments. Piles of this gravel were sold at US$25 a load. It took a family about one month to break down and gather a single pile. These were the lucky ones. Like the farm labourers on the vast sisal, maize and tobacco plantations, they had an income, meagre but sufficient to keep starvation from the door of their shanty homes.

Over the years, I have often been invited by schools, businesses and organisations to give slide shows and talks on my expeditions. During these talks, I have never tried to conceal the harsh reality of life for many people in the poorer regions of the world. My intention is not to invoke pious pity but provide a reminder of the gross human inequities which we must all struggle to remove.

Out of the hardship great nobility and beauty also comes. Our visits to the villages of the Chagga and Masai tribes brought us in contact with proud and hospitable people. Some of the mud huts of the Chagga sported TV dish aerials. Inside whole families sat on dirt floors. Apart from the TV set flashing magic images, conditions had not changed in thousands of years.

The huts with generator-fed televisions are usually the homes of safari or Kilimanjaro climbing guides. It was both amusing and annoying to consider that their extra income was spent not on anything of real domestic value. But maybe that is too western a viewpoint. The escapism provided by television is, for many Africans, their only respite from a tough and austere way of life.

The Masai are markedly different and, despite generations of colonial rule and burgeoning western influence, their customs and traditions have remained largely intact. This tall, strikingly handsome brotherhood struggle to live as nomadic cattle herders. But over-population and the consequent demand for land and living space has constricted their movement.

The creation of vast wildlife reserves has also led to considerable conflict between Masai and officialdom. They regard themselves as a caste higher than fellow blacks and whites and are very often shunned by Africans eager to embrace the western way of life. Working with the *mzungu* (foreigner) appears not to have lessened their obduracy or affected their tribal distinctiveness and separateness. Many Masai families have been forced to settle and cultivate the land. These *shambas* or small farms are invariably poorly maintained by people who have an inherent difficulty being anything other than pastoralists. This aversion to agriculture is deeply-rooted in the ancient Masai religion.

We lived with Simba's sister in one of the small and claustrophobic mud huts – home to two adults and six children. Diana sat in the dark, smoke filled hut before a fire. Her breasts hung below her knees like the mammaries of a much older woman. At 18-years of age, she was the youngest wife of a 60-year old Masai elder and had already borne him six children. On her back she carried her youngest baby. Every time it cried out she cupped one of her sagging breasts, lifting it shoulder high to meet the hungry mouth of her child. Diana's husband had five other wives and each of them lived in their own hut in this typical harem compound. The women would bear children for as long as they physically could – this was the tribal way of life.

I could well understand why Africa has one of the fastest growing populations on earth. By the turn of the twenty-first century, the number of people living on this continent will have doubled. There is little that can be done about this as tomorrow's parents are already born.

Over-population and the inability of the land to support such numbers of people means that tomorrow's children will be considerably worse off than their impoverished parents are today. That is one aspect of Africa, another is its phenomenal natural magnificence.

Oh! the garden of eden has vanished they say,

But I know the lie of it still ... go the lines of the popular Irish Percy French ballad.

This song came to mind when our jeep drove over the lip of the Ngorongoro volcanic crater. This 20 km wide crater is a veritable immense bowl which contains just about every primary species of wildlife to be found in East Africa.

From the crater rim we could view a vast tract of wilderness all around. Below in the grassland plains were lions, elephants, rhinos, buffaloes, wildebeest and zebras and many other species we would encounter in the coming days. In the midst of all this wildlife Masai, who have grazing rights in the crater, tended their herds.

In 1978 Ngorongoro was declared a World Heritage Site, fifty years after the first road was laid across its unspoilt tapestry of plants and animals.

Camping under the stars during our wildlife excursion, which also included Tarangire and Lake Manyara, we savoured the sights and sounds of this natural paradise. Hugely impressed by the whole Africa experience I decided there and then to plan a return visit. This happened quicker than I expected and the following year, Joe and I would lead an expedition of Irish climbers up the beautiful and challenging Machame Route to the summit.

On that particular adventure, I was joined by my good friend Nashu Maruki from Turkey who was climbing Kilimanjaro as part of his Seven Summits Challenge. The second journey to Kilimanjaro was to raise funds for the Irish Rehab Foundation, an organisation which operates training programmes for people with special needs. The Irish team ranged in age from 17 to 59 years, from diverse backgrounds and professions. They all had one common ambition – to visit Africa, most to climb Kilimanjaro, others to walk the African plains and, in doing so, raise money for a worthy cause.

Eleven of the team would walk cross-country in the company of Masai to climb Ol Donyio Lengai – an active volcano and the holy mountain of the nomads.

By the time the remaining 33-strong group headed off from Machame village, our team consisted of the Irish gang, one Turk and a 'small' 50-strong army of Tanzanian porters headed by Tobias, our guide on the mountain. The positive attitude of the team seemed to turn the mountain into an enormous energy field that drove everyone upwards towards the summit. The porters had wagered bets against the whole final team reaching the summit. They lost.

I will never forget the expressions of joy on the faces around me as we congratulated each other on the summit. For Jim Farrell from Limerick, his ambition to climb Kilimanjaro was driven by the most intense emotion. Jim's father, on his death bed some months earlier, had asked his son to carry a stone from his grave to the summit. His father had always had a burning desire to visit Africa but had never realised this dream. Jim took his father's memory and a stone and placed it next to the wooden plaque marking the top. He then picked a stone from the summit to bring back and lay on his father's grave.

For me, standing on Kilimanjaro in 1996 was one of the proudest moments in my life. I had been here before. I had even climbed Everest. But this was special, different – for, by my side was my seventeen year-old son, Brian. We had had our difficultues over the years – lengthy periods away from home in the course of my travels had strained our relationship. I desperately wanted Brian to accompany me on the African trip. Americans call it 'quality time'. I don't know if that means anything. All I wanted was to spend time with my son in what would be a shared adventure and something I deeply hoped would bring us closer together.

Family history can often be mirrored in your chldren. As a teenager I regarded my father as being a bit of a bollocks when our views on certain matters failed to dove-tail. Now, I felt that Brian looked at me in a similar, jaundiced light. This was especially true when, many weeks before our departure, he asked me if I thought he would reach the summit of Kilimanjaro.

'Because it's such a high mountain, I'm not certain I'll reach the top. You never know how the body will react to high altitude,' I responded.

This was misinterpreted by Brian as a put-down.

'Dad, why are you always trying to make me feel small? You don't think I am capable of making it to the summit. Do you?'

With great difficulty I attempted to explain that I was being truthful and honestly could not say who would make the top and who would fail.

'Getting to the top should not be your only objective. Take it easy and look forward to visiting a country which has so much to offer. If you get to the summit let that be a plus,' I told him.

In Africa, Brian opened his heart and his mind and soaked-up every moment of the experience. I found his to be invaluable assistance when organising the day to day activities of the team and he showed great leadership qualities. But Brian thought he would never make it as we scrambled up the physically demanding final stage of the Machame route where many of the team suffered blinding headaches and severe nose bleeds caused by the high altitude.

With steely determination he silently, steadily soldiered on and as I stood proud of his achievement on that hallowed summit he turned to me, grabbed me in a spontaneous hug, kissed me and said – 'Dad, you're a weird fucker but I love you.'

ON TOP OF THE WORLD

Ships in a harbour are safe,
But that's not what ships are built for.

John Shedd

It takes the best part of sixty days to walk to the top of this earth – eight weeks, most of it spent jousting with the fear of the unknown in a place where man was never meant to survive. I remember vividly the sickening, gut-knotting feeling I had in my stomach in March, 1995, as I packed my gear for my second attempt on Everest. Feelings of excitement were mixed with an intense anxiety, realising that I might not return to the comfort of my family and friends.

Weeks before my departure, fears – many of them irrational – haunted my sleep. I tried desperately to suppress my sense of uneasiness and maintain a calm demeanour. The history of Everest is punctuated with tragedy. I knew the risks and, in 1993, experienced, first hand, the death of a climbing friend, Karl Heinze.

My departure from Cork Airport had a funereal air to it. People were crying and hugging me as if I was about to embark on a journey to the 'other side'. My mother, a devoutly religious woman, pinned an emblem of the Holy Spirit on my lapel. 'Wear that at all times, son. I know the Holy Spirit will protect you,' she said giving me a bear hug.

Once airborne, I began to concentrate hard on the task ahead – there could be no room for self-doubt, no wasted energy on negative thoughts. A wiser mountaineer than when I first attempted Everest, this time I believed I would succeed if given a fighting chance.

Kathmandu was again the meeting place for those in the 1995 expedition. While here I spent a number of days with my old Sherpa friend Tsiring and his family. Before leaving Tsiring's home to join the other members of the team, he took me to a Buddhist temple where he and close family members prayed for my success and safe return. I needed those prayers. The flight from Kathmandu to Lhasa in Tibet I thought would be my last.

145

The aircraft was sucked into a vortex of turbulence as it struggled to maintain altitude over the Tibetan plateau. Looking out the port-hole I could see the wing flex at least six feet upwards and downwards and waited, frozen with terror in my seat, for the damn thing to suddenly snap-off. The plane was diverted to Changdu in China and over the next three days the pilot of this high mileage commercial carrier would make two attempts to fly through the troubled air to Tibet and the highest city in the world and home of the exiled Dali Lama.

Under Chinese occupation Lhasa has become a mere silhouette of its former and glorious self. It is now a tatty place apart from the Patala, the former home of the Dali Lama and place of worship for the Buddhist nation. Patala sits on an elevated site atop the otherwise dreary municipality.

From Lhasa we travelled by jeep across the barren, largely featureless Tibetan plateau and for the next three days bone-shook our way to the foot of our zealous objective.

Base Camp was established near the Buddhist monastery at Rongbuk on the glacier of the same name. This would be our new

The 1995 Everest expedition with members from nine countries.

146

home away from home, a place which we would leave and return to many times as we made the switch-back climb to and from the various camps stepping up the mountain. This back-breaking approach of climbing high and sleeping low had a two-fold purpose – it enabled us to acclimatise our bodies to high altitude and stock the camps with supplies for the climb to and from the top of Everest.

It can take years of planning, training and personal sacrifice just to get to the Everest starting point. And for what? To spend far less than one hour, in many cases just mere minutes, standing on a wind-whipped barren mountain head of snow and ice six miles high in the sky. The allure of this mountain is difficult to express, especially when you are sitting outside your tiny dome tent in the early morning light and gazing at its imposing silhouette against the brightening sky of a new day.

Looking at this wonderous monument to the might of nature, I could not help but question the wisdom of risking limb and life to declare – 'I did it'. What did Karl mean when he said he felt an 'energy' drawing him to this place as he orbitted the earth in his shuttle?

For many years I had remained in a state of infatuation with this mountain. I too had felt the spiritual draw of some obscure terrestrial force. It was like being hopelessly in love with an elusive woman. The only way I could turn this unrequited love into something fulfilling was to struggle upwards and reach her most sancrosanct place – the summit. Those who have gone to the mountains will know how difficult it is to rationalise the desire of men and women to take it to the limit. They also know that it far transcends a craving for success – the drive to plant your foot, your flag or both on that lofty goal. Mountaineering is so much more than that. It is about meeting people from all walks of life and all corners of this planet. It is about broadening horizons of perception, coming in contact with different cultures and social structures and from that, acquiring a wide-angle vision of this world in which we live.

British mountaineer John Hunt, who played a major role in the historic endeavour to conquer Everest in 1953 wrote, after Hillary and Tenzing's glorious achievement – 'The story of the ascent of Everest is one of teamwork. If there is a deeper and more lasting message behind our venture than the mere ephemeral sensation of a physical feat, I believe this to be the value of comradeship and the many virtues which combine to create it. Comradeship, regardless of race or creed, is forged among high mountains, through the difficulties and dangers to which they expose those who aspire to climb them, the need to combine their efforts to attain their goal, the thrills of a great adventure shared together ... if it is accepted that there is a need for adventure in the world we live in and provided, too, that it is realised that adventure can be found in many spheres, not merely upon a mountain, and not necessarily physical.'

Comradeship has meant so much to me during the planning and execution of each and every one of my expeditions. Without it, none of my exploits would have ever reached fruition.

My return to Everest in 1995 was filled with anxiety. I knew the enormity of the task before me but this did not erode my determination to stand on the highest point on earth, and to bring with me the symbol of our country and emblem of our traditions and culture, the Tricolour, to the highest point on our planet.

As I sat there day-dreaming my Sherpa friends and team mates began their day's activities and before long Base Camp took on the aspect of a busy ant hill. One week after establishing ourselves at Base Camp the weather had improved considerably and we were finally beginning to leave our foot-prints further and further up the first stages of the mountain. Before we made the initial trip out of Base Camp, monks from the nearby Rongbuk Monastery and our Sherpas performed a *puja*. To a makeshift altar of stones strings of prayer flags were anchored. This reminded me of my childhood in Cork and the bunting which people hung from their homes in celebration of the Corpus Christi church holiday. A wooden pole rose from the centre of the altar and to this the monks had attached a *khata*, or white ceremonial scarf, and a sprig of juniper. Some juniper branches were also burned on the altar as the Sherpas and Buddhist monks prayed to the gods of the mountains that we would be spiritually re-born and cleansed of our sins. The prayers, gladly, were for good weather and fortune in our expedition also. And to ensure our success sacrifices of grain and butter were made and rice and water scattered in all directions. It was now up to the gods whether or not to accept our offerings and grant us safe passage through their lofty sanctum.

As I stood and prayed in my own way my thoughts again

turned to the death of Karl. En route to Advance Base Camp, some time later, I had tried to find his grave and pay my respects but I failed to locate the stone marking his final resting place.

At this stage I had teamed up with the 22 year-old Australian, James Allen. We would climb together for the rest of the expedition and this proved to be a mutually beneficial arrangement as he and I were of similar personality and temperament.

By early May the weather was calm enough to enable our expedition's first successful summit bids – James and I were pencilled-in to make our first stab at the top on 16 May.

On that date we were brimming with energy and confidence as, for the third time, we pushed our way to Camp Two at 7,900 metres (26,000 feet). There we would rest, as best we could, for the night and the following day climb to High Camp and then to the top. It all seemed so simple, so straightforward, so uncomplicated until later that afternoon when a storm cloaked the mountain with a suddenness which sent a shiver down my spine. Jet stream winds, in excess of 100 miles per hour, came shrieking upon us

Looking out over Changtse from Camp Two on Everest.

149

with sphincter-tightening force.

Our tiny nylon dome tent, which was precariously tied to a rocky outcrop and looked insecure enough before the weather had turned cruel, felt as if it would be carried away at any moment with James and I enveloped inside – an air mail parcel sent from Camp Two to God knows where. The fabric stretched under supernatural stress and the thin alloy ribs flexed and sprung in all directions. We lay there in a state of shitless high anxiety unable to move and not knowing how long this barrage would last. Our primary worry was that the tent would be destroyed at any second – these shelters may be lightweight and seemingly flimsy but without them survival would be impossible at high altitude and in bad weather. For two long windy days we remained trapped. Then, as suddenly as it had been born, the wind died.

'Let's just make the 8,000 metres mark Pat and leave it at that – we'll never reach the summit now.'

'I have a better idea – why don't we drop down, get some rest and food and give it another shot. I think we can still make it to the top – I do.'

Tired and utterly exhausted we dropped to Base Camp, two weather-vanquished souls. Had we gone to 8,000 metres we would have placed ourselves at considerable danger as the break in the bad weather was momentary only and, while unoccupied, Camp Two was completely destroyed. After some days rest we were on the move again, Camp Two having been re-established by other members of the team in true 'all for one, and one for all' spirit. James and I advanced to our previous highest point on the mountain and prayed the weather would be our ally.

At 10am on 26 May, 1995 we left our tents and headed for High Camp and into the 8,000-metre plus 'Death Zone'. Long-range meterological forecasts gave us approximately three days to get to the top and off the mountain before Everest's upper reaches were struck by a series of storms. Deciding it was better to travel as light as possible when making the final assault, we left our sleeping bags at our last camp and put every faith in our quality one-piece down suits, said to be good for temperatures as low as minus 40 degrees Celsius. But we were both chilled beyond the bone.

We rested in these impossible conditons of cold, hunger, thirst and inadequate oxygen levels. My crowded thoughts passed through the blender of my subconscious – visions of avalanche, rockfall, home, family, friends, triumph and failure danced in my cluttered head. Suddenly, I was roused from a half sleep when it looked as if the door of the tent was collapsing on top of us.

Quickly I unfastened the door and peered outside. Lying on the snow, on our door-step, was expedition member Bob Hemstead.

'Holy God! – you look knackered. What the fuck happened?'

I dragged his large Alaskan

Bob Hemstead, whose slip near the summit was nearly fatal.

frame into the tent and after a brief recovery period he told us of his epic adventure at the summit. When just fifty metres from the top he slipped on the hard ice of the slope he was climbing and rocketed off, head-first, down the way he had come. Speeding down towards the Great Northern Couloir like shit off a hot shovel, he tried but failed to self-arrest his slide with his ice axe and tumbled out of control. Eventually he managed to snag himself on a small outcrop of rock, which stood on the edge of a 1,000 metre vertical drop.

'I clung here, looking down into this nothingness and bawled my head off for help. Man I can tell you I had more to fear than fear itself.'

Like a giant multi-coloured bat he hung on, upside down, as two of the summit party that day, Greg Child and Sherpa Ang Babu, somehow managed to put a few pieces of rope together and throw them to Bob as he stared bug-eyed into the icy abyss below him. With slow, careful dexterity he tied the rope to his body and was pulled to the safety of the upper slope. Shaken and shocked, Bob and his rescuers made their way to the summit. As he stood on the crest with a fractured hip, he performed the highest cowboy rope trick in the world. Bob's Alaskan cowboy dream was to perform his rope act on the highest mountain on each continent of the world.

The climb to the summit had been far more demanding than

anything Bob had envisaged. His account of what had happened emphasised the acute danger of the whole exercise.

Listening to Bob, our confidence to press onward and upward became eroded – as the night wore on and the wind rose, my mind became cluttered further with positive and negative thoughts, 'to go, or not to go'. Retreating would have been the easiest option but I had worked many years to get to this point and, hopefully, higher still. Since early afternoon, I had boiled six litres of water and we ate our carbohydrate concentrates, washed down with rehydrating liquid.

I tried to get some sleep in readiness for the tough climb ahead but I just kept twisting and turning and found it impossible to relax – a fact which must have annoyed James and Bob. It was a long and largely restless night. The winds grew in intensity and made unsettling, howling noises around our flimsy shelter from the merciless elements. My thoughts again turned to the deaths of Karl Heinze in 1993 and Mick Reinberger – who summitted in 1994 on his seventh Everest expedition but never returned home to tell the tale.

Just across from us, another two of our expedition members, professional climbers Mike Smith and Brigitte Muir, had made camp in the late afternoon and their target was the summit also. If successful for Brigitte, this would be her last seven-summit attempt to become the twenty-third climber in the world to accomplish this feat.

At this juncture I felt we had to go for the summit or retreat. I could not spend another night in that mental no man's land, not knowing whether the next stage of the expedition would be going up or coming down. The hand set of the radio crackled with static life causing a nervous jolt to run through my fatigued body – it was Mike Smith calling from his tent.

'Come in Pat, come in James.'

'Pat here, come in Mike.'

'The temperatures are dropping and the winds are picking up. What do you and James intend doing?'

It was decision time. I looked at James with wide open eyes. He looked back at me with a similar beaming expression. We had held out against blasts of jet stream winds and temperatures which would knock the balls off a brass monkey. We didn't have to discuss our next move. I knew what James was feeling and, like me, his adrenalin was starting to course through his body. We might have been freezing cold but our focused ambition burned with a warming intensity. In a synchronised movement, he and I raised our thumbs upwards – a silent gesture which left us in no doubt about our intentions. We were going to the place which has for generations preoccupied the dreams and aspirations of mountaineers – the top of Everest. Neither of us wanted to relive the disappointment of our summit attempt a week earlier when we were pushed back from our 7,900 metre camp.

I reached for the radio handset, cleared my throat and with a quiver in my voice said – 'Come in Mike, we're going for it, what do you and Brigitte intend doing?' After a brief pause, Mike answered –– 'We'll be across shortly.'

Then came another call from another nearby camp – Russell Brice, who was leading a sister expedition, informed us that one of his team, Miko Valanne from Finland was going to attempt the summit as well and would be leaving at the same time as us.

'Is it okay if he joins you?'

It was, and at midnight, 26 May, 1995, five of us headed into the dark abyss of the cold night. The question on everyone's mind was 'can I do it?'

This was the most challenging part of the expedition to the summit of our dreams. Here, we would need the ability to move over treacherous rocks which were angled in such a down-sloping way as to give no secure foothold to the climber. On the roof of the world, with a fall-off of thousands of feet on every side, we struggled to maintain mental equilibrium and to remain calm, composed and confident of our ability to cope with the lack of oxygen and overcome the many obstacles in our path. Our bodies were under enormous pressure, both mentally and physically – this was the ultimate test of man against mountain.

All my fears and anxieties were cast into the deepest recesses of my mind. I clicked into positive mode, completely focused on the task ahead and with the steadfast frame of mind of *'I CAN DO IT!'*

We were now trudging slowly and ponderously up the most dangerous section of the climb at over 8,000 metres (26,000 feet) – the 'Death Zone' – using head torches to light our way. Our first objective was the sharp-edged crest of the North East Ridge which rises slowly to the summit and is broken by three formidable barriers known simply as 'The Steps'.

Severe cold gnawed through our layered protective clothing adding to the sheer misery of climbing in this unwelcoming place. Nonetheless we were feeling good as we pushed our way up the North Ridge to begin a traverse to the First Step. This barrier lay between us and the most perilous section of the climb – a seventy degree gradient chute of snow, ice and rock.

The conditions were deteriorating in the endless night as we made our cautious approach to the First Step. This was the very slope where George Mallory and Andrew Irvine were last seen before they disappeared on 9 June, 1924. I felt a chill enter my bones which was somehow not related to the temperature.

The five of us were well spread out along the route and looked like a string of sleep-walkers as we slowly, laboriously picked our way under the dim light of our head torches along the twisting course punctuated by rock sentinels. Fingers and toes numb with the cold, we reached the bottom of the First Step, the obvious place to regroup. It was 3am and Mike, James and I made our first radio contact with Base Camp telling them of our position on the mountain.

John Muir, who took our call, asked about the progress of his wife Brigitte. We informed him that we were awaiting to regroup with her and Miko who were bringing up the rear. Twenty minutes later, standing in the raw cold, there was still no sign of her or Miko. The ground to this point was relatively easy and posed no technical challenge. We assumed that they had turned back for reasons which could not have been serious and we informed Base Camp of our intention to continue.

To our horror we later discovered that Brigitte, who had become separated from Miko, had been blindly climbing this section after her head torch gave up the ghost. In the minus 40 degrees Celsius temperature the cells of the torch had expired. She replaced the dead cells and the same thing recurred. While she attempted to resuscitate her head-lamp, she lost visual contact with James who was ahead of her on the twisting ridge. Frustrated at her predicament and feeling she had been robbed of her summit bid, she waited in the freezing cold night until first light before descending to High Camp. Feeling fit enough she planned another attempt the next day. Miko also returned to High Camp later that morning having abandoned his summit attempt. Neither he nor Brigitte were granted an audience with Chomolungma, not this time.

Exiting the top of the first major barrier on the upper section of the mountain we began the long and precarious traverse to the next rampart – the Second Step.

While on this spectacular traverse – on an extremely nerve-wracking apex where the force of gravity seemed to pull me from the incline – I was finding it naggingly difficult to climb with my oxygen mask. I constantly fiddled with it and eventually moved it to the side of my face so I could see where I was placing my feet as we made our way to the 'Step. Still blinkered, I shut off the flow and took off my mask. This seemed to have little impact on my performance. At 6am, we arrived at the most demanding section of the climb – the notorious Second Step and the famous aluminium ladder that had been erected by the Chinese on the 30 metre high crag of intimidating rock in the 1970s. I may not have needed a full blast of oxygen earlier but now I figured things were about to change. Quickly, I reconnected my oxygen supply. This stage was far more demanding than I had imagined and called for a few tricky moves along an arête and into a type of chimney in the rock face before reaching the ladder.

Making my way from the traverse onto the knife-edged arête, I put my boot on a big loose boulder, about four foot square, which shot out from under my feet and hurtled past James, just below me, before breaking into a myriad of fragments which cascaded thousands of feet down the North Face of Everest. Nervously, I made my way up the small gully which channelled us to the foot of the ladder.

The ladder was fixed to the sheer rock face to assist tired climbers overcome a vertical obstacle which has prevented many mountaineers from claiming the ultimate prize. It dangles there, precariously, and while it is a God-send, it is nonetheless a nerve-fraying experience to alight the climbing frame which sways in the wind, left and right and in and out, above a seemingly bottomless drop.

As I gained each rung on the 20-feet ladder, I wondered if I would be the unfortunate climber to pull the ladder from its stressed and rusted anchorage pins in the rock. Hanging there, halfway up, I glanced far below to see the body of a dead climber snared on an icy outcrop. We believed these to be the remains of Mike Reinberger, a stark reminder that getting to the top was only half the job. Still focused on the task and knowing that there was nothing I could do for the climber that lay in an eternal grave just below me, I stepped off the upper rung of the ladder.

At this point it was necessary to make a very tricky move to the right to get to the safety of the upper slope and continue a traverse. As I looked up, the summit stood there, alluringly beautiful but nonetheless a symbol of man's frailty in this forbidding place. I uttered a prayer for the climber below and thought of Karl Heinze.

At the top of the Second Step, Mike and I stood there on a damn steep part of the climb waiting for James. As James started to climb, he put his weight on one of the old fixed ropes leading to the ladder, gently at first and then gave it a heavy tug. It broke loose from its anchor and James started to stumble backwards. He reached out with his left hand and just managed to grab another fixed rope and somehow pulled himself upright. At that point he spotted the dead body below him. I could sense he was gripped with fright. However, he continued climbing up the rock face, traversing along the gully and around a few boulders to the edge of the ladder. Near the topmost rung, James got into serious difficulty. The ladder was swaying in an alarming fashion and James seemed to be unable to step off.

I was feeling extremely cold and exposed. I sucked a deep breath of oxygen from my bottle and felt its 'hit' immediately. It was still early morning and the wind chill penetrated our layers of clothing. I could feel my fingers and toes getting increasingly numb and no matter how much we tried to keep them warm by swinging our arms across our bodies, rocking back and forward, wriggling our toes inside our boots, walking in place, nothing worked. A few minutes passed as James endeavoured to gain the ledge to the upper slopes. I was unable to help him as we were not roped together.

'Pat, if we don't move off now we'll get frostbite. Tell James to make the move or go down. He's got to do one or the other – we can't stay here all day.'

James and I had been together since the start of the expedition and it was breaking my heart to see he was so close but that he might be forced to retreat. The summit was within his gaze if not his grasp. But the sight of the expired climber on the slope below him had spooked James into a spell-bound state of sheer terror. He tried to muster the courage to commit himself to the move from the top of the ladder to the top of the exposed crag knowing that one mistake, one hand or foot wrongly placed, would have fatal consequences.

'Come on James you can do it,' I shouted from my exposed perch looking down on him.

'Fuck! Falvey I can't make it. I can't make it.'

I could see the agony in his face as he looked beyond me to the summit only two hours away. Would our sixty-day struggle end this way with my climbing partner unable to climb any higher?

'Come on James, you can do it.'

He tried again and responded with the same words of exasperation as he struggled to step from the swinging ladder onto the narrow and critically exposed rock ledge. Mike and I were getting colder, a lot colder – dangerously cold.

'Pat, we'll have to go – we can't stay here much longer,' Mike urged me.

I made one more attempt to encourage my stricken friend.

'Come on, James, we're freezing here – we've got to move.'

James tried again, but failed. He looked up at me and I could see the emotion in his tear-filled eyes as he roared – 'Fuck it! Falvey ... I can't ... you go.'

Tears welled in my eyes. There was nothing I could do. Mike and I hesitatingly started to walk away leaving James still at the top of the ladder, dejected and seemingly unable to climb any higher. Leaving my friend to return down the mountain, I felt quite distraught. But this was something we had discussed earlier – the inability of one to continue should not hinder the other's attempt to summit.

Mike and I trudged up through an easy slope, where the gradient had lessened, to the Third Step on the ridge. All I could think of was James' plight and frustration at being so close and yet so far from realising his dream. As we made our way towards the third barrier the morning light became brighter and brighter.

Looking down from this heavenly observatory into Nepal and Tibet, enchanting landscapes appeared through breaks in the light cloud like dark-room images developing on photographic paper.

With every few tired steps, I glanced back in the hope that James would be there. I felt guilty at the thought of having left him to go down alone, and his expression of hopelessness remained etched on my mind.

157

Turning one last time to glance down the slope, I thought I was witnessing an apparition. It was James coming up behind us. He had executed his giant leap and was with us on the final leg of our epic journey to the summit. This was going to become a perfect ascent after all. Elatedly, I called out to Mike some metres ahead on the snow slope and we waited for James.

'Pat, I think I have frostbite on my fingers,' were the first words James uttered.

'How the fuck did that happen?'

He explained that to make the move off the ladder he removed one of his three layers of gloves for a number of seconds. But this was no place to take off his gloves and check. In any case, he wasn't too perturbed and just pointed his finger towards the summit. He was not turning back now. No way.

Later, James would lose the top of two digits as a result of severe frostbite which affected both hands.

Looking at James I was reminded of how close he had come to seeing his dream shatter before his eyes. Placing my hands on his shoulders, I pulled him towards me, gave him a bear hug and declared – 'let's go for it!'

Mike and I shared James' concern over the fact he was suffering from suspected frostbite but the three of us, pumped full of adrenalin, continued quickly above the Third Step. From here, we made our way across the final snow slope onto the rock band leading to the crest of the summit approach.

This was it. The last few hundred metres to the highest place on earth – out onto the summit slope which seemed to be supported by the high, puffy clouds. I was now about to cross the highest platform on earth. I was thinking of how, millions of years ago this place would have been at sea level. There is clear evidence that rocks which lay on the bed of the earth's deepest ocean underwent a powerful thrusting upwards and fossil remains of sea creatures had been located in the rock strata above 8,000 metres on Everest. As I walked on this narrow ridge with the world below my feet I tried to comprehend the events, the time and power involved in the creation of this place. It baffled me.

A feeling of excitement rose from the pit of my stomach to fill my heaving chest. Only 100 metres to go. Delirious with undiluted joy I began to sing and hum – *Oh! I do like to be beside the seaside ... beside the seaside ... beside the sea ...*

158

The last fifty metres below the summit.

Approaching the last fifty metres, my emotions were running riot. These few minutes were the most amazing moments of my life. Step by step by lingering step, I inched my way to the top. I began to feel as if my soul and body had somehow parted company.

But when I look up the white road
There is always another one walking beside you
Gliding wrapped in a brown mantle, hooded
I do not know whether a man or a woman
— But who is that on the other side of you?

Those haunting lines from T S Eliot's 'The Waste Land' later came to mind as did the extraordinary, super-human achievement of Ernest Shackleton who, at the turn of the century, led a 600-mile trek across Antarctic ice and ocean. In the final days of that heroic trek, Shackleton believed his team had been joined by a mysterious, spectral presence which walked with them to safety. I too felt a strong spiritual nearness which sent my heart racing. It was as if my subsconscious floated somewhere above my head and viewed my final journey from on high.

There is no height, no depth, that the spirit of man, guided by a higher Spirit, cannot attain.

Remembering those words of John Hunt, I now knew exactly what he was talking about. Tears of joy streamed from my eyes and froze on my beard as the awesome Himalayan chain started to unfold below. Glaciers which, for hundreds of thousands of years, have been slipping down the sides of these enormous rock formations, lay spread out on all sides like the fingers on the welcoming hand of the 'Goddess of the Earth'.

I will never forget the last few steps and there I was, standing on top of the world. I could have roared with joy but instead I silently prayed. Thoughts of those who had gone before me, and sadly those who never completed the journey back to Base Camp, ran through my mind.

James, Mike and I just stood there in silence for a minute and turned 360 degrees to take in the greatest view on this earth. Then we looked at each other and with clenched fists rose them in the air and roared out. 'Yes, we've done it. We're standing on top of the world.' I remembered what my father had always professed. 'Dream and dream big but remember ... it's in trying to make your dreams a reality that the success lies'. My dream had now become a reality.

I fell to my knees. 'Thank God,' I uttered.

At that glorious moment in my climbing career, I reached my hand into my breast pocket and took out my Irish Tricolour. This, I tied to my ice axe clenched in my fist and held it high with pride. I felt as if I was standing on a podium at the Olympics after winning a gold medal. I could hear the National Anthem ringing in my ears. I trembled, as surges of adrenalin gushed through my body. There were tears running down my face from the intense emotion I was feeling.

It was quiet and peaceful as I stood on that patch of sacred ground, six miles high in the sky. There were no television cameras, no press and no roaring crowds to distract me. The time I spent there was very beautiful and gave me a personal, inner satisfaction that was calming and private. I was excited and elated beyond description. I was so proud to be an Irishman standing on the summit of the Goddess Mother of the Earth.

James came forward and took my photograph holding the Tricolour on the roof of the world – my most treasured souvenir. In turn I took some shots of Mike and of James who was then, at twenty-two years of age, one of the youngest climbers to ever summit Everest from the dark side – the Mallory-Irvine Ridge.

With a snake-like hissing sound I was brought back to reality.

160

My oxygen bottle had run dry. Most of the deaths on Everest occur on the descent and oxygen run-out was a causative factor in many fatalities.

'I'll have to go down now. I've run out of oxygen and I don't want to get hypo-toxic.'

My stay on the summit was too short lived. I stood there for a few seconds more and savoured my time with Chomolungma and then began the long walk home. I thanked the God of the mountains and every God for giving me the strength to stand there and I prayed for my safe return. Saying farewell to James and Mike, who were going to stay for another little while, I turned and started my descent.

Feeling fear and intense anxiety, I walked alone down the summit slope to the first rock outcrop.

'Come on Falvey – don't fuck up now. Make the right decisions, the right moves – concentrate, concentrate,' these words ran through my head like a mantra.

On our return, the Second Step became the scene of high drama yet again. The descent can be considerably more difficult than the upward climb. And our exit from Everest was no exception. Mountaineers who have focused their entire mental and physical resources on reaching the top have very often paid a dear price for paying undue attention to the rigours of the return climb. Just before the Second Step, oxygen deprivation and fatigue were stamping my resolve into the snow when I remembered that my Russian friend, George Kotov, had left a half bottle of oxygen there. Making it to the Step, I found George's bottle, plugged into it and sucked the life-giving gas, not realising that just a few hundred feet above me a crisis was unfolding.

Mike was in a very bad state. His oxygen had also run out and this was having a serious effect on him. He was hypo-toxic – a build-up of carbon dioxide in the lungs – and also showed the savage signs of pulmonary oedema in the space of just a few short minutes.

James told me later that he thought Mike was about to die, there and then when his eyes began to roll back into his head and he kept falling in and out of a hypnotic sleep. His drive to survive was not fully diminished and with a stumbling motion, Mike eventually made it to the top of the physically and mentally demanding Second Step. Swaying on his unsure feet, he stood before me gasping for breath and barely able to talk. Before the pair arrived at the 'Step, Mike had radioed for help saying he was dying and required oxygen. Frantically we searched the upper slope of the second step to try and find another stashed oxygen bottle. James and I checked a few bottles dumped on the snow. Eventually we found one which had a little gas left in it and plugged this to Mike's breathing set. He recovered a little. I knew then the only way to save his life was to get him below the 'Death Zone'.

'Come on – we'd better get out of here.' I made my way to find the elusive exit onto the Second Step and the ladder. After about three minutes I had found it. I was lucky. Climbers have perished here unable to find the cleft in the ridge – the only way to the ladder and relative safety.

I clipped to the fixed rope running down the ladder and made a speedy descent. As I was coming off this section, with the other two still high on the crag, I spotted a person making his way across the traverse to the Second Step. As he drew closer, I recognised the solitary figure as Niama, one of our Sherpas, who was answering Mike's call for help. Niama had volunteered to climb from our high camp at 8,200 metres (26,900 feet) with bottles of oxygen. This, for me, was further illustration of the stamina and steely will of these extraordinary mountain folk without whom few expeditions could succeed on the Himalayan peaks.

Niama and I stood here at the bottom of the Second Step as James began his descent of the Second Step. Before leaving, he clipped Mike into the fixed rope and then walked to the edge of the cliff face that overlooked the whole, seemingly bottomless north face. Exhausted and unable to hold his own body weight on an abseil, he just let himself slide down the rope until he came to a knot which stopped him from going any further. He hung there for a few seconds working up the enthusiasm to swing across to the ladder. Clenching the side of the aluminium frame with one hand, he unclipped from the rope and crawled down the ladder, slowly descending the small gully at its base and over the arête to the traverse where Niama and I were now clipped in.

'Come on Mike, it's your turn,' James roared above the wind.

Lying slumped over some rocks at the edge of the Second Step, Mike slowly rose to his feet. He then slid down the fixed rope, to which he had been pinned, out of control and at speed. His full weight juddered to a halt at its end. It held fast, somehow.

'Damn that was a close one. Too fucking close.' I could see the tension in James' and Niama's faces.

He then somehow tapped enough reserve energy to make it onto the ladder. From there he seemed to slide, limply to the bottom and very slowly made his way down to where we waited. Niama climbed some fifteen feet towards Mike with a bottle of oxygen and rigged it up for him. He sucked deeply on the mask and, after a few minutes, started to move again and made his way over the edge of the rock arête and down to the traverse at the bottom of the step. What should have taken only five to ten minutes had now lasted over an hour. Mike was in serious trouble.

Niama clipped Mike into the fixed line that made its way to me. I was about forty feet away from them. Mike moved like a drunken man, his eyes heavy and his movements unsteady as he approached James and I. He was having difficulty staying on his feet and we were about to execute the most potentially hazardous part of the descent. I remained very conscious of the dead climber just below us. A shiver of fear ran through my spine at the sight of Mike as he started to move. It was as if he was sleep walking. As he moved on the traverse my worst fears were realised.

'Oh! Jesus Christ. No,' I uttered as Mike's feet suddenly slipped and, as if in slow motion, he went skating some nine feet down the fifty degree sloping rock face.

I instinctively grabbed the fixed rope knowing that if the full pressure of the fall came onto the piton behind me, it would pull it loose and Mike would be lost. Niama, on the other side of Mike, did the same. As he fell he displaced some loose rocks. I watched them cascade thousands of feet down the mountain. If the piton pulled or the rope broke, Mike would take the same course as those rocks into the abyss below us. Mike's fall came to a halt. He looked like a discarded string puppet spread-eagled on the slope. I roared at Mike to get back on his feet and up to the traverse, only feet above.

He nervously edged his cramponed boots onto the rock and in an exhausted state reached for a hand-hold. As he tried desperately to pull himself up, he slipped again, just having struggled to his feet, and slipped further still.

'Oh Christ. He's gone.' My eyes shut tight as I feared for the worst. But the rope was tight in my hands. Again he was prostrate on the sloping rock and looked as if he had finally given up. He lay here with his face buried into the crook of his arm, motionless.

'Get back on your feet, on the rock!' we shouted in a desperate bid to motivate him.

Again he pressed the crampon teeth of his boots up against the rock and made his way back onto the traverse. Shock and the early stages of pulmonary oedema were toying with his mortality.

Once back on the ledge, we sat him down. He was coughing blood and finding it almost impossible to breath. Had he a punctured lung? We prayed this was not the case. We had to get him down as quickly as possible – nothing else could save him now.

I went path-finding. James followed behind with a sling attached to Mike and Niama behind Mike again attached by a similar sling. Our progress was punishingly slow as we started to descend the long traverse across the north-east ridge to the top of the First Step.

Here a second Sherpa, Dorgi, arrived and he took over from James. Then we all started a slow, exhausted drop. The more we descended, the more alert Mike seemed to become. On arrival to our high camp, Russell Brice, the sister expedition leader, had brews on for us. Would anything taste as good ever again?

Mike was put to bed in his tent where he was kept under constant supervision.

Russell had been preparing to go for the summit the following day with Brigitte but due to the changing weather conditions he had changed his mind. We were to be the last climbers to summit on Everest that season.

After consuming as many hot drinks as my bladder could hold, I retired for the night and fell into a swift and deep sleep. The following morning all I wanted to do was stay in my bag and sleep some more. But with great determination Russell made sure we all got up and started to move down the mountain. We were spending far too much time above the 8,000 metres 'Death Zone'. The expedition was far from over. There was a lot of mountain below us to negotiate. Mike was still on emergency oxygen and looked very weak as we made our way down to our 7,900 metres (26,000 feet) camp.

From there, it was one long slog onto the North Col at 7,076 metres (23,000 feet). With each step my boots were becoming heavier and heavier until it felt like I was dragging anchors. After every few steps, Mike had to stop, doubled over by a retching cough.

164

Phlegm dribbled from his chin. Jesus! he looked like death. There was no way he could possibly make it across the glacier at the foot of the North Col. This was going to be a struggle for James and I but for Mike, an impossibility.

I radioed to our Base Camp leader and asked him to provide support at the foot of the North Col.

Mike, James and I made our way down the fixed ropes off the North Col onto the glacier below to be met by four Sherpas sent up from Advance Base Camp with flasks of hot tea.

More importantly, they provided the muscle and energy need-ed to get Mike down. He had made a superhuman effort to get this far and he deserved to survive. Drained and worn out from the long slow descent from the summit, I also had to contend with severe sunburn which affected my face, the inside of my nose and pallet of my mouth. The latter is a mountaineering pit-fall. When you are panting from breathlessness, the UV rays reflected from the snow underfoot hit the inside of the mouth and the result is the most painful sun-burn imaginable.

It was great to have the support of the Sherpas for the last few kilometres to the safety of Advance Base Camp.

James and I walked ahead while Mike, assisted by four Sherpas, followed slowly behind. But, just as we approached Advance Base Camp, a radio call from Ang Babu reported that Mike had collapsed.

Twelve climbers and Sherpas went to the assistance of Mike and carried him back to Advance Base Camp. He was placed in a Gamow Bag – a form of decompression chamber for extreme cases of pulmonary oedema – and treated by our expedition doctors. Diagnosed as hypo-toxic, with a punctured lung and oedema he had one foot inside death's door.

Inherent strength and a steel will to survive, coupled with expert medical attention, saved this man's life over the next few weeks. Mike had been blessed – another couple of hours at high altitude and his name would have been added to the ever-growing roll of brave men and women who have perished on Chomolungma. These were harrowing days which came at the tail end of an experience I will always remember as I made the final assault on the highest mountain on earth. 27 May, 1995 will remain with me as the best day of my life. In the past twelve months I had reached the highest summit on three continents.

Mike Smith being attended to after his return from the summit.

Back at Base Camp champagne corks were popped and after copious drinks of wine and the best part of one litre of good Irish whiskey, which I had saved for this moment, the agony of the expedition turned into sheer ecstacy.

As we were celebrating the success of our crusade back home my family and friends were in a state of great distress amid media reports that I was feared missing on the mountain. This had arisen due to a communications breakdown between Base Camp and home. The media knew, roughly, when I was expected to summit. But, when I was on top of Everest our satellite telephone system at Base Camp malfunctioned cutting us off from the outside world.

Over-zealous members of the media interpreted the silence from Base Camp as a bad omen and ran with reports to the effect that I was missing. Eight days of silence came in the wake of my summit success – I was so relieved when I finally reached Kathmandu and was able to telephone my family.

In Kathmandu I bade my farewells to Tsiring and his family. Before going, he took me to some of the local temples to give thanks to the gods for my success and safe return home.

Looking out the window of the jet I could see the forty shades of green tapestry of the Irish countryside – I was going home. Sitting next to me were a honeymoon couple who wanted to know everything about my homeland. Ten minutes before our scheduled arrival a message came over the plane's intercom – 'would Mr Pat

Falvey please make himself known to one of the crew.'

Slightly embarrassed and wondering what this was all about, I held my hand aloft. A young lady stewardess leaned across the seats and held out her hand. 'Congratulations, we just received a radio message from the control tower at Cork Airport informing us you were on this flight. Well done!'

She asked me to stand at the rear of the plane once it had touched down. This I did as over the intercom came the captain's voice once more – 'Ladies and gentlemen, we are honoured today to have on board Mr Pat Falvey who is returning home having climbed Mount Everest. On behalf of Aer Lingus, the crew and myself I would like to congratulate Mr Falvey.'

Then, my fellow passengers rose to their feet and, turning towards me, applauded. The blood rushed to my face in a beaming blush.

Making my way along the tarmac towards the arrivals' gate I was met by a gang of family members, friends and press, radio and television journalists. I was hugged, kissed, hand-shook and back-slapped into a state of total euphoria.

Airport personnel directed me to the VIP lounge where I was met by local politicians, including the Minister for Sport, Mr Bernard Allen, TD, and a battery of media people. Balloons, flags and 'Welcome Home' banners bedecked the room.

In the midst of the throng I picked out the faces of Marie, Brian, Patrick, my sisters, brothers and my mum.

As for my dad, well, a passage was cleared through the crowd and as press photographers snapped away merrily he walked towards me wearing his formal chain of the office of the Lord Mayor of Cork, Councillor Tim Falvey.

'On behalf of the people of Cork may I congratulate you on your extraordinary achievement,' he said with feigned formality. Then he wrapped his arms around me, kissed me on the cheek and said – 'well done, son. You have made us all proud. Well done.'

THE STONE SENTINEL

I see the Gaucho crossing the plains, I see the incomparable rider of horses with his lasso on his arm, I see over the pampas the pursuit of wild cattle for their hides.

Walt Whitman

I awoke to the relentless flapping of the tent in the wind which never became anything more forceful than a strong breeze. It remained with us all the time, chill and dry, sweeping through the gaps in the Andean mountains and down the arid valleys. No other sound could be heard apart from the friction of the tent's inner membrane against the outer sheet.

'What was that?' muttered Con as he poked his half-awake head from his sleeping bag.

'Just the wind.'

'Whose wind is what I'd like to know,' he said accusingly.

'Well, what will it be for breakfast? I know. Let's have fried eggs.'

'No. Why don't we try cooking them in a pan in some pre-heated oil,' Con quipped.

'Wait a while. Why don't we scramble them in a pan of hot oil.'

'No, too fussy. Let's just have them fried.'

'Okay so. Fried it is. Would you like them well done, not well done or in between.'

'I'll have them in between, in between two large slices of freshly baked bread, that is.'

And so began another clear day on the trek to Aconcagua, 6,962 metres (22,841 feet) which straddles the border of Argentina and Chile and is the highest mountain in the western hemisphere. The only fresh food we carried with us were three dozen eggs which are not all they are cracked up to be if you have them every morning for breakfast.

Con Collins and I arrived in Buenos Aires on 13 December, 1995 after a non-eventful 29-hour journey from home. We booked into our hotel, had something to eat and went to bed. The following day we left the city for Mendoza which, basking in the warm

168

South American sunlight, was a pleasant city of tree-lined boulevards populated by beautiful people. The women were especially lovely with dark hair, brown eyes and sallow skin.

We organised our climbing permits, bought food for the expedition – including the three dozen eggs – and booked a muleteer and three of his beasts of burden. Feeling we deserved a little recreation before resting, we hired a taxi to take us to a roadhouse outside the city which had been recommended as a good traditional place for a few pints.

Chilean immigrants singing their native songs.

The bar stood in the middle of the desert some fifteen miles outside the Mendoza city limits. Alighting from the taxi we asked the driver to return and pick us up in two hours. Inside the spartan watering hole we got into conversation with a smiling bunch of Chileanos who had come to Mendoza in search of work. They reminded me of the Irish who, through the generations have been forced to migrate to Britain and the United States of America and, like my countrymen, they were eager to sing after a few drinks.

Con and I matched their Chilean folk songs with some of our favourite Irish ballads and the time slipped by, unnoticed. Our taxi driver entered the bar while we were at the height of our ribald delivery of the 'Boys of Fairhill'.

Come and have a holiday
With our hurling club so gay
Your souls we'll charm and your hearts,
We will thrill.
The girls, they will charm you
The boys they won't harm you
Here's up 'em all says the Boys of Fairhill.

The subtleties of the song may have been lost in the alcohol fuelled heat of the moment but the Chileans nonetheless went wild with applause and bought another round of drinks. It is impossible for an Irish person to turn his or her back on a good session and Con and I were no exceptions. We paid the taxi driver $20 and asked him to return later.

At 2am Con tapped me on the shoulder. 'Pat, we have a wake up call at 8am and our taxi driver hasn't come back yet. Let's go – we might meet him on the way.' The party, we reckoned, would probably last for another few hours at the rate it was going. We said our farewells, wished our new friends all the best and gave a farewell song – 'As I leave behind Neidín', written by fellow Corkman Jimmy McCarthy. *'Won't you remember, won't you remember, won't you remember me. As I leave behind (Mendoza).'* Singing the final verse as we waved goodbye, we staggered out into the cold desert night hoping our taxi driver would turn up or we could thumb a lift to Mendoza. The desert road was, well, deserted.

Four hours later we had made it to the hotel, totally shagged. No sooner had my head hit the pillow, or so it seemed, when the telephone rang. 'Hello Mr Falvey – this is your 8am wake-up call.'

Struggling from bed I blearily made it to the shower. Con struggled also to face the new day and make ready for the mountain. Over breakfast our plan to begin the trek to the mountain was put on hold when I ran into some British climbers I had climbed with in Scotland and Tibet.

'Care for a few drinks later?'

I looked at Con. Con looked at me. Nothing was said. We ended up doing a tour of the bars in Mendoza and had great *craic*, again. The unscheduled drinking spree was deeply regretted the next day when we rose from our beds feeling decidedly *craw-sick* – a fitting Cork expression for an horrendous hangover.

Rolling along Highway 7 in a Peugeot estate taxi, taking us to the ski resort of Los Penitentes, we enjoyed the conversation with our driver Carlos Machado. Portuguese by birth, he was a direct relation of the poet, Antonio Machado. I knew as much then about Machado's poetry as I do now about quantum physics but this was something which caught the interest of Con.

Carlos had worked for many years as an electrical engineer in Paris but felt that life in a 32nd-floor city centre apartment with his wife and children was less than ideal.

Once we had booked into a local hostel, Carlos suggested we visit Puente del Inca, some six kilometres east. A ruined church and disused buildings stood like bad teeth against a desolate, arid landscape. It reminded me of the locations used in Italian western movies of the 1970s.

The taxi man took us to a cemetery for *andinistas*. The majority of those interred there had perished on Aconcagua. We discovered the grave of Nicolas Plantamura, who made the first Argentine ascent of the mountain in 1934. I prayed there was nothing prophetic about the fact that our first sighting of the mountain was made while we stood in that sombre place.

The mountain has been called many things by many people. I recall a reference to 'an intolerably monotonous slag pile' in one climbing guide. But from where we stood, more than fifty kilometres away from its foot, it looked daunting and impressive, standing high above the lesser mountains and foothills in its company. Since the 1980s, it has become a much sought after prize among the climbing fraternity of all nations. In excess of 1,000 climbers attempt the summit most seasons with an average success rate of 30%.

In latter years the mountain – which translated from the Quechua words *ackon* (stone) and *cahuac* (sentinel) means 'Sentinel of Stone' – has been referred to also as 'the dump heap of South America'. In 1990, park rangers staged an extensive clean up of the waste discarded by expeditions to the mountain. More than eight tonnes of trash were removed from the Horcones Valley approach alone. After many hours deliberation, Con and I had decided to take on the Polish Glacier Route to the top, so named in 1934. The route, first blazed by a Polish team, ascends a prominent glacier on the sweeping north-east slope of the mountain. If the feedback we received from recent climbers was anything of value, this route had all the promise of ice, snow and crevasse-dodging thrills.

At Punta de Vaca we rendezvoused with Ricardo de Torres, our muleteer. Ricardo was an authentic gaucho, dressed in characteristic style with waistcoat, hat and scarf. He carried his lasso, knife, tobacco and *maté*. The gauchos traditionally were cowboys, the sons of conquistadores and settlers with Indian or negro blood. Ricardo farmed 40 acres for most of the year and supplemented his income by ferrying loads on the mules for the climbing season. His main ambition was to get enough money to send his eldest son to university to study law.

From Punta de Vacas at 2,325 metres (7,628 feet), we began the

Ricardo loading for the trek to Base Camp.

long hike to the park ranger station at Las Lenas. The landscape on all sides of the steep river valleys, which channeled our approach to the mountain, was arid and largely bereft of vegetation and wildlife. At Las Lenas we approached the stone walled, tin roof hut of the ranger's outpost. He checked our permits and issued us with plastic refuse sacks which we were expected to return full at the end of the climb.

We camped for the night at this spot and chatted amicably with the ranger who, outside the climbing season, worked as a chef in a Bavarian restaurant. The night sky was spectacular. Here in the wilderness and away from the influence of urban street lighting, the heavens became one of the most marvellous sights in nature.

We arose next morning to another clear day, breakfasted on eggs and broke camp early. Our next stop was the shelter at Casa de Piedra at 3,200 metres (10,500 feet) and at the end of a long haul up the Rio de las Vacas. Water levels in the river were surprisingly low. According to our gaucho muleteer, Ricardo, the past few years had produced very little rainfall in the mountains.

The track was rough and much of the time we picked our way along the steep, stony banks of the river. We finally made our next camp and that night, after dinner, we sat around our camp stove boiling water for abundant cups of *maté* – a tea-like, sugar-laced beverage with a slightly tobacco flavour which Argentinians drink in enormous quantities.

Next day we followed our mules up the extremely narrow Relinchos Valley to our Base Camp at the 4,200 metre (13,780 feet) Plaza Argentina. En route to Base Camp, one of the mules, for reasons known only to itself, spooked and bolted. Con – no stranger to ornery critters having been brought up in a farm environment – and Ricardo managed to retrieve and calm the nervous beast. I was almost glad of this temporary distraction from the monotonous hike to Base Camp.

Without the mules, the walk-in would have been quite arduous and maybe even impossible for Con. Just a few days before we left Ireland, Con was horsing around with his children when he put his back out, badly. Damaged ligaments at the base of his spine bent him like an S-hook and for a time it looked as if he would be unable to make the Aconcagua trip. Con's younger sister Teresa, a practitioner of an ancient Tibetan form of energy healing called Reiki, gave him an intensive course which aided his recovery dramatically. But he was still apprehensive about the carrying which we would have to do without the aid of mules from Base Camp upwards.

At Base Camp, we took a day off and spent most of it eating and drinking. It was five days before Christmas and our thoughts turned to home. We shared the moraine campsite with some other climbers, some of whom we got to know quite well in the short time we were there.

Early on 21 December we loaded our packs of provisions and gear and headed off for Camp One at 4,700 metres (15,400 feet). Con was carrying a slightly lighter load but still enough to aggravate any lingering back problem. The carry went well over rough moraine and icy scree. The last 500 feet up the glacier were, as Con frequently pointed out, 'brutal'. We were both gasping for air and quite exhausted when, almost seven hours later, we reached Camp One, which rested in the shadow of some high and precipitous rocks.

We stayed for over an hour, stashed our gear and returned to

Base Camp. The most memorable but also punishing aspect of the 'carry' to Camp One had been our journey through a steep field of *penitentes* – a wind sculpted ice formation said to look like white habit-clad monks at prayer. Picking our way through the *penitentes,* there were occasions when I thought we did not have a prayer of finding a passage through this bizarre formation of man-sized, ice statues.

22 December began bright, clear and calm. We emerged from our tent feeling rested and ready for another trek to Camp One with more gear.

'Do you know what Con, I really feel like a breakfast of eggs.'

'Funny you should say that. I was just about to suggest the same thing. We haven't had eggs for ... jaysus! it must be nearly 24 hours.'

'Come on so, let's get cracking.'

At least we could still laugh about it. But it was nearing the point where the very thought of an egg was enough to turn us both anorexic.

That night was the first we spent at Camp One. After dinner and bedded down for the night Con produced from his rucksack a booklet of Irish ballads. For the next hour and a half, we stridently worked our way through most of the songs. Two American climbers from Seattle camped nearby may have thought this behaviour strange as the still, snow covered mountain echoed the cacophony of our combined voices.

Don't forget your shovel if you want to go to work
Oh! don't forget your shovel if you want to go to work
Don't forget your shovel if you want to go to work
Or you'll end up where you came from like the rest of us – digging –
Ow di diddle do ...

Christmas Eve was spent at Camp One but this was not a day of rest. I dropped to Base Camp to collect more gear while Con headed in the opposite direction and took a load halfway to Camp Two atop Ameghino Col at 5,380 metres (17,650 feet). That evening we reunited at Camp One where we were joined in our small dome tent by three Californian lads, Eugene, Carlos and Edo. From the bottom of my rucksack I produced some tinsel, a model of an Aer Lingus jet – to remind us of our return journey home – and other little festive decorations. A mini bottle of Bailey's liqueur was divided five ways and we sang 'Silent Night' more than once – much more.

On Christmas Day, the sun rose in a clear sky. Deep snow, after a night of incessant fall, covered everything in a glorious, glistening, white blanket. Despite it being a traditional feast day, our Christmas Day breakfast consisted of eggs again. Dinner was somewhat better when, after some instantly forgettable dehydrated con-

Eugene Cordero, from California, who suffered from the altitude.

coction, our Californian neighbours produced a tin of fruit cocktail for dessert. We celebrated the holiday lazing about, resting in our tent and singing our heads off. From this day on, through most of the remainder of the climb, the weather took on a set pattern – from early afternoon each day it snowed heavily.

Over the next few days we did carries to Camp Two at 19,700 feet (5,900 metres) at the base of the Polish Glacier, our chosen route. On 26 December we noticed, on our return to Camp One, some new arrivals had made camp nearby.

We were invited into the tent of an American climbing couple. Every item in the tent was labeled either 'Bill' or 'Tammy'.

Hot water was brewing on the stove and mugs were passed around. After our hard day's climb, Con and I were gasping with thirst. Bill picked up a plastic container, which had his name emblazoned on it, and from it took a tea-bag. Tammy was handed her personal tea stash. But Con and I were given mugs of plain hot water, just that, as the couple picked our brains on the climb ahead.

On 27 December, the blizzard was relentless and lasted all day. Con and I took turns to dig our tent out at regular intervals. The following day, we dug our way out and, after a breakfast of, I think it might have been eggs, broke camp. We trudged onwards and upwards to Camp Two. Above us on the glacier, the signs were ominous. There was no suggestion of the new fallen snow settling and the featureless and tilted Polish Glacier looked like the head of

175

a giant snow shovel about to dump its load – on us.

Here we encountered other climbers who had decided to drop down and find a potentially safer route. We too conceded defeat, sort of. Deciding to retain as much height as we could manage, we opted to traverse from the foot of the glacier, near Camp Two, and pick up the 'normal route' on the North Face of Aconcagua. It was a punishing traverse through knee-deep snow from the glacier, across mixed ground to our campsite at the aptly named 6,000 metres (19,680 feet) White Rocks.

Our tent was lashed by a merciless blizzard throughout the night and neither Con nor I were sorry to be on the move early next day through a break in the weather to our destination, the summit. Surprised by how easy it was to pick-up the trail to Refugio Independencia at 6,546 metres (21,476 feet), we got stuck in with an enthusiasm which psychologically kept the coldness at bay.

The Independencia hut, which is now in ruins, was built in 1951 and named after Juan Peron. It was said to be the highest alpine refuge in the world and a welcome sight to many summiteers too cold and exhausted to make it back to camp without a breather.

From here our next goal was the Canaleta – a 400 metre, thirty-three degree chute of snow littered loose rocks and scree. This was regarded, by those who had gone before us, as the most taxing part of the climb. I remember it as a series of twists and turns over steep, unsure ground and around each turn the energy-sapping sight of yet another steep slope to scramble up.

Eventually, we came out on top of the Cresta del Guanaco which takes its name from a large and reclusive wild mountain goat, the guanaco, one of which we were fortunate to sight days earlier.

We rested briefly. Before moving on, we were joined by Eugene, the only one of our three Californian friends who felt able for the final stage to the summit. Looking at his drawn facial expression and hearing his heaving breathlessness, I felt Eugene should have stayed behind with his colleagues. He looked drained of all energy and complained of dizziness. Leaving Eugene sitting on the ridge, after he had assured us he would be okay after a brief rest, we went for it – the summit.

There is nothing more aggravating than knowing the top is well within reach but having a nagging feeling in the pit of your stomach that you will not have the vitality to carry you those last few hundred feet. Traipsing along the final stage of the ridge rising gradually to the highest point, I began to feel a billowing sense of excitement and achievement.

It was 3.30pm on Sunday, 31 December, the last day of 1995, and we had realised our South American dream. What a way to celebrate a New Year's Eve – to be standing on top of the highest mountain in the Western hemisphere. I hugged Con, Con hugged me. We took photographs, ate our summit treat of chocolate bars and, denied any decent views by snow clouds, began to retrace our steps.

Before leaving the summit, Eugene arrived on the scene, panting, his legs buckling under him – in a word, fucked.

He staggered towards us with his head in his hands. 'Oh Jesus! I've never felt so bad in my life, I'll never make it back down,' he wept as he fell to his knees and crumpled up in the foetal position, in pain and feeling the effects of altitude sickness.

'Would it be okay if I joined you?' he pleaded like a lost child. There was no way he could have made it safely back down the ridge and we had no intention of abandoning a stricken mountaineer. Our descent was reduced to a crawling pace as we assisted Eugene through the deep snow on the Cresta del Guanaco ridge back to the col between the summit and its lower sister peak to the south. With his hand resting on my shoulder he followed like a blind man across the ridge. On numerous occasions he collapsed to his knees, exhausted and spirit-broken. We somehow reached the col. It seemed to have taken forever. Now we had to negotiate the most dangerous part of the descent down the Canaleta.

While climbing down a rock step on this section Eugene, who was still directly behind me, tumbled forward in an uncontrollable cartwheel. As he came somersaulting over me he struck the back of my head with his ice axe. He fell to the ground in front of me and I jumped upon him before his tumble gathered deathly momentum down the steep slope.

'Jesus Christ, we'll never get him down without a rope.'

We sat Eugene in the snow and discussed our worsening predicament as the afternoon blizzard grew in intensity.

'There's only one thing to do – one of us will have to drop down quickly and get help, and it's not going to be Eugene,' Con said and I agreed.

So, I volunteered and left Eugene in Con's care as I began my descent, as far as was necessary, to get help.

'I know what I have to do but I have no control over my movements,' were the last words Eugene spoke to me as I left him with Con.

While I made ponderous progress through an emerging snow storm back to White Rocks, Con emptied Eugene's rucksack and dressed him in all the spare clothes he had packed and sat him in the shelter of a rock. Not long after my departure Con was joined by a Canadian woman guide. Four Spaniards, returning from the summit with her, refused to help but Catherine did the honourable thing and proved to be strong and resourceful. She suggested getting Eugene to squat into his rucksack. Then she took the loops from their ice axes and tied those to the 'sack.

With Eugene looking like a bag of potatoes, Con and his Canadian accomplice – who were also joined by two Swiss climbers we had met days earlier – slid him down the slope, holding on to the nylon 'reins'.

Meanwhile, I had reached our camp at White Rocks and informed Carlos and Edo, Eugene's partners, of the crisis. With them I continued to Camp Berlin where we hoped to radio for assistance to the ranger's office lower down on the mountain. There, feeling totally dried out, I drank a litre of fluid and headed back up the mountain with Carlos and Edo. Higher up Con and the others came to a halt at a section where an almost horizontal traverse was called for.

Strapping two ski-poles to the improvised rucksack sled they pulled, shunted and shoved Eugene inch by inch and eventually reached the relative safety of the derelict shelter at the 6,546 metre (21,476 feet) Independencia Refuge.

The lower Eugene was dropping the more he was recovering. After a little rest at the derelict hut he believed he could make the rest of the journey unaided. Catherine and the two Swiss climbers departed quickly while Con and Eugene made slow but steady progress towards our camp at White Rocks. We met Catherine and she told us that everything was under control so I asked her to make sure that the rescue call I had made from Berlin Camp was cancelled. She assured me that she would.

At White Rocks I was re-united with Con and Eugene where we retired to our respective tents to celebrate the New Year. Con and I had a few shots of Irish whiskey, which we had been saving throughout the trip. Exhaustion, coupled with dehydration, resulted in me being totally knocked-out by our celebratory tincture.

I awoke at 2am on New Year's Day believing I was hearing voices in my head crying, 'Falvey, Falvey – where are you?' It must be a dream, I thought. But the call persisted. 'Falvey, where are you?'

Hesitatingly, I shook Con. 'Listen, do you hear a voice?'

'I do – yours. Will you go back to sleep.'

'Seriously, Con. Listen. What do you hear?'

Con sat up and, sure enough, he too heard the plaintive cry above the wind. We unzipped the flap of our tent and shone our head-torches into the cold, dark night. 'Fuck it – it's Willie,' said Con in wonder at the familiar face caught in the beams of our lamps.

Willie Vinegas, a professional climber and guide we had become acquainted with in Mendoza, spends six months of every year leading groups to the peaks of the Andes. With two other climbers Willie had answered my rescue call, unfortunately.

'What the fuck are you doing here, the rescue was called off,' I said.

'Oh shit! We didn't know. Our radio went down just after we picked up your alarm call. Well, we're here now. How is your man? I hope his insurance is in order, 'cos he's going to get billed for this rescue,' Willie said matter-of-factly. After checking with our American friends that they were okay, they headed back to Berlin camp.

Con and I snuggled back to the comfort of our sleeping bags and duly fell back into a deep sleep. Two hours later Carlos' head poked through our tent door. He was concerned about Eugene's health. 'Pat, Eugene is in a frantic state and we're worried that his condition is worsening. Could you take a look?' Raising from my warm cocoon I went to check him. He looked like shit. He complained of having no feeling in the extremities – he was breathing heavily, could barely talk, had a splitting headache and his complexion was yellow. It was evident that he was once again suffering badly from high altitude sickness and required immediate evacuation to lower altitude. I got Carlos and Edo to get Eugene ready. Twenty minutes later Eugene and I began the long descent to Base Camp, while Con, Carlos and Edo would break camp and follow later. As we descended, Eugene made a mircaulous recovery. Later that evening we all joined up again for a belated New Year's celebration.

On 3 January, having said goodbye to the climbers at Base Camp the previous day, we checked-in our rubbish bags with the ranger at Las Lenas where we would camp for the night. Our food supply was exhausted. When the 'ranger invited us to dine with him, we were thrilled. In his hut, we sat chatting as he threw tender Argentinian beef steaks on a hot pan.

'Smells good. *Muy bien.*'

'The meal I will cook is popular here. It is called *el bife a caballo* which in your language means "steak on horseback". You fry your steak and on top of each one you place two fried eggs, *dos huevos.*'

Ah! the good ol' *huevos*, I thought. We were right back where we started from, geographically and gastronomically.

Back in Cork, some weeks later, Con and I met for lunch. He produced a report from a mountaineering magazine, *High*, which added spice to our ascent of Aconcagua.

'... the Aconcagua Provincial Park report that the high winds and extremely cold temperatures of the 1995-'96 austral summer have made reaching the summit via the Normal Route a matter of survival.

'The usual success rate on the line is around 30 percent but this season, unconfirmed estimates suggest that it may have dropped to two or three percent.'

WAR-TORN CAUCASUS

To scorn all strife, and to view all life
With the curious eye of a child.
From the plangent sea to the prairie,
From the slum to the heart of the Wild.
From the red-rimmed star to the speck of sand,
From the vast to the greatly small;
For I know that the whole for the good is planned,
And I want to see it all.

Robert Service

The news on the car radio related the Kremlin's determinaton to pound Chechen separatists into the rubble of the capital, Grozny. This was the culmination of a three-year independence bid by one of the many non-Russian nations scattered along the Caucasus mountain system which stretches from the Black Sea in the north-west to the Caspian Sea in the south east.

For the past number of months I had been following the news dispatches from Chechnya, adjacent to my destination, with particular interest. This morning, however, my mind was merely half-focused on the radio bulletin.

'What if he's not there? What will I do then?'

'For God's sake, Pat, will you relax.'

'Go a bit faster.'

'Oh! be quiet and stop shuffling. If I go any faster, we'll be arrested.'

I was getting on Joe's nerves. Early on the morning of 16 March, 1996 my close friend was driving me to Shannon Airport and I was driving him around the bend.

'What time is it now?'

'It must be all of ten minutes since you last asked.'

The cause of my anxiety was, not that I might miss my Aeroflot flight to St Petersburg, but the prospect of failing to make a crucial rendezvous with a truck driver on the main road near the airport. The boot of the Volvo contained almost all the gear necessary for my assault on the highest mountain in Europe. I was missing one

181

vital element however. In the province of Kabardino-Balkaria, where the mountain is situated, I had decided to cross-country ski. I had never skied before and, consequently, I did not possess a pair of cross-country skis.

My efforts to find a store in Ireland which stocked these came to naught. Con Moriarty, through his Mountain Man store in Dingle, managed to locate a supplier in the UK and a pair were duly ordered.

There was some delay in shipping them to Ireland so here I was, the morning of my scheduled departure for Russia, hoping to meet the delivery truck on the side of the road near Shannon.

'That must be him. Quick, pull in.'

I hurriedly got out of the car and approached the driver sitting in the parked lorry.

'How's it goin'? I'm Pat Falvey. Have you a package for me?'

'Pleased to meet you, Pat. But I'm afraid you have the wrong man. I just stopped to have a cup of tea and a bite.'

'Sorry to disturb your breakfast,' I said dejectedly and walked back to the car, cursing under my breath.

One hundred metres up the road, we pulled in alongside another parked truck.

'Are you Pat Falvey?' enquired the driver before I had a chance to say anything. 'I have a package here for you. I hope you're going travelling, 'cause you won't find much use for skis around here,' he quipped.

Not bothering to unwrap the delivery, I placed them across the back seat and jumped back into the car. 'Let's go, Joe – Elbrus here I come.' At 5,633 metres (18,480 feet), Mount Elbrus is the jewel in the Central Caucasus.

On St Patrick's Day, I was in the company of my Russian climbing friend and Everest partner, George Kotov, his wife Irene and his young daughter Masha. The snow-covered, architecturally-impressive city of St Petersburg belied the easy-going and non-cosmopolitan nature of its inhabitants. The Russians I encountered were so very much like the Irish – warm, friendly and hospitable. The Irish national holiday was celebrated in grand, vodka-fuelled style. We did not merely wet the shamrock but rightly soaked it in an Irish pub called Molly's.

When it was my turn to buy a round of drinks I walked to the bar. 'Are you being looked after, boy?' said the barman in an unmistakable Cork accent.

'Well, you're not Russian,' I declared.

'Excuse me, I'm going as fast as I can,' he said jokingly.

Christy, the barman, had lived in Cork just 200 yards from my parents' home although we had never met before this. We discussed mutual acquaintances and the drink flowed freely, on the house that is.

For four days, George took me on the grand tour of his beloved city and I abandoned all preconceived thoughts of the Russians being a drab and dreary race. But did they feel suppressed by officialdom despite the fact the authorities claimed to be embracing the policies of *glasnost* and *perestroika*? I put this question to George.

'Pat, recently a friend of mine was asked the same question by an American. The American said: "I would hate to be Russian, you don't even have freedom of speech." "What do you mean?" said my Russian countryman. "Well," added the American, "I can stand outside the gates of the White House and shout – 'the President of the United States is a dick-head" and nothing will become of me. "So what?" said my Russian friend. "I can stand outside the gates of the Kremlin and shout – "the President of the United States is a dick-head" and nothing will become of me. So, it would appear we enjoy the same freedom.'

Small and slightly-built, this chain-smoking, vodka-quaffing character is one of the most fun-loving climbers I've ever had the pleasure to meet and I eagerly looked forward to the days ahead.

On the flight from St Petersburg to Mineralnyye Vody, George and I also recounted our experiences in Scotland and the Himalaya and discussed the climb ahead.

The war in Chechnya was attracting the focus of the world media at this time. The epicentre of this internal unrest was distant from Elbrus but the military authorities had become unsettlingly wary of all outsiders. For almost a year-and-a-half Russian troops and Chechen separatist rebels had been locked in bloody warfare. Over 50,000 people – a conservative estimate – would perish in this bitter feud before the Russian President, Boris Yeltsin, and Chechen leader Zelimkhan Yandarbiyev, would convene peace talks.

During my time on Elbrus, the Russian bombardment of the capital, Grozny, was in full swing. Despite the terrible loss of life, the Chechens remained resolute. 'We are not part of Russia. The Russians may kill and conquer us but they can never force us to be something we are not,' was their collective *cri de coeur.*

On hearing these fast-held views, I was reminded of the conflict in Northern Ireland.

'Pat, at the checkpoints remember whatever you say – say nothing. Leave the talking to me.'

'No problem, George – I don't speak Russian anyway.'

On arrival in Mineralnyye Vody, we hired a Lada car and driver and headed off towards the Baksan Valley leading to the foot of Elbrus. Before long we arrived at the first of many check-points. The soldiers looked cold and bored. Alex, the driver, rolled down his window and began a seamless stream of idle chatter with the guard. Occasionally, the soldier looked beyond George towards me. I smiled, oafishly.

With ease of movement the driver took 10,000 roubles, about the equivalent of US$2, from his pocket and handed the cash, which I had earlier given him, to the soldier.

The conversation ended and we were waved on. 'These guys are paid so little they would starve to death if they could not collect bribes.'

There was military presence everywhere. The driver told us that since the conflict in Chechnya there had been far more troop movements than was usually the case. Hundreds of vehicles lined the roadways outside Mineralnyye Vody as the check-point guards took their time filtering each means of transport and, more importantly, their contents through the martial net. Most of the cars, trucks and buses were travelling from Russia to Georgia via Kabardino-Balkaria and the troublesome Ossetia. Fearing attack by the many militias and Mafia gangs that control the roads here, people would pay the sum of 150,000 roubles to the Russian military for an escort of safe passage to Georgia.

The Caucasus has remained a redoubt of people whose allegiance is to family and clan. Some 50 different languages are spoken across this snow-capped neck of mountains separating the Eurasian seas. And there is always a struggle going on for room, influence or independence. At each and every check-point, the graft changed hands. I was not too concerned by this – the sums paid in back-handers were minimal and we were in turn saved a lot of time-wasting, bureaucratic bullshit. But meddlesome officialdom dropped on me like a tonne of civil servants on our arrival at the hotel in Cheget, adjacent to Terskol, a popular holiday resort for military personnel.

The village of Cheget is situated at the upper end of the Baksan Chaussee and is used as the principal base for all excursions in the Elbrus region. Here we had planned to spend some days while I mastered the art of skiing.

The registrar at the hotel warily checked my papers and passport. Then, with the expression of somebody who could turn the contents of a samovar to ice just by looking at it, declared – 'you do not have the required permit for the Central Caucasus. You should not be here. How did you get this far?'

He knew the answer but this, unfortunately, was not a hint that his palm could be greased also. George, despite his cheery banter, gave me the distinct impression we were dealing with the Russian equivalent of a bollocks – somebody who was going to follow the law to the letter and cared little for mountaineers or any other species of foreigner.

'You can spend the night here. I will keep your passport, money and luggage. The customs officials will be informed of this and tomorrow we will see what will happen.'

Depressed and miserable we went to the allocated room. I had the distinct feeling that the next day, I would be shown the door out of Kabardino-Balkaria.

The marketplace in Cheget which reminded me of my grandmother.

'It's not his fault, George,' I said of the registrar from hell. 'I should have waited until all the necessary permits came through.'

'What you need is a drink. We will worry about tomorrow when it comes.' And, with that, he pulled a bottle of vodka from his bag. This man could produce bottles of booze the way a magician could rabbits from a hat.

Arriving in the foyer the next morning, having had little sleep, I was beckoned to the desk. 'There will be a car to take you to the customs office in Tyrnyauz.'

George accompanied me in order to act as interpreter and I was glad of his moral support. The drive to the town of Tyrnyauz left little impression on my memory. On the way, my thoughts were focused on my doubt that I could ever climb all seven summits – would Elbrus be shielded from me by a wall of yellowing paperwork?

We entered the spartan offices of the customs officials and were ushered into what looked like a cell. It smelled of stale cigarette smoke and fresh body odour. Behind a plain desk sat a grey-suited, cigarette-smoking official. He waved his hand towards the chairs opposite and left a trail of cigarette ash across the papers spread out before him.

Looking at me with an unemotional expression, he said, in broken English: 'You should not have entered restricted area without necessary papers – understood?'

His accent was thick, his skin I suspected even more so.

'It is mystery how you got as far as you did.' Bullshit, I thought. Here is a man who has probably taken baksheesh on occasion – he knows the score.

'What you have done is very serious, most serious. Can I see your passport please?'

I passed him the passport into which I had slipped a $50 bill.

He flipped the pages, stopped at the bill and gave me a look which said – 'you have made a mistake, a big mistake.' I had misread this man and he was insulted by my presumption that he could be bought-off.

'You will be escorted to back to Mineralnyye Vody. This is as far as your visa will allow you to travel. You must pay fines also.'

Just then, I felt like somebody had unscrewed my toes and the spirit of my adventure was draining from my body. Before I got a chance to say anything, George began speaking with a rapidity which I thought should have been beyond the scope of language, even Russian. Looking at the official's face, I eagerly tried to read from his expression what George was saying to him – but his face remained blank.

George kept up his tirade for what seemed like an eternity. I understood none of the one-sided conversation, though at one point I thought I recognised a familiar name – that of the soccer supremo Jack Charlton – but felt I was mistaken. The man in the suit just sat there. Then suddenly, George stopped, the official rose to his feet and extended his hand towards me.

'Let me wish you best for your adventure. Good luck on your climbing,' he said with a smile. This turn about in attitude made my head spin.

Outside the customs offices, I heartily slapped George on the back. 'How did you do it? What did you say to him?'

Lighting a cigarette, he took a deep drag, tilted his head back and blew a small mushroom cloud into the air. Then a coat-hanger smile spread across his face.

'I began by telling him about your ambition to climb the seven highest mountains on the seven continents, explaining to him that you came from Ireland – a tiny island in the Atlantic.

'When this failed to register, I happened to add that Russia recently played a friendly soccer match against Ireland and that your national team was managed by Jack Charlton. And was I glad to discover that he was a huge football fan who knew Charlton's reputation as both a player and manager,' explained George with not a little smugness.

George further explained that the official was miffed by the failure of the Russian embassy officials back in Dublin to provide the necessary permits when the application which had been sent to them plainly stated my desire to climb Elbrus.

A native of Kabardino-Balkaria, he was all in favour of attracting tourists to the region where unemployment had become a major problem. He was unable to stamp my passport but expressed the desire that the climb be completed successfully and without military intervention. I was warned that if stopped at a check-point the military would take a dim view of the fact that I did not have official permission to go beyond Mineralnyye Vody and, if discovered, would be deported. This was a chance I was willing to take.

The next few days were spent on the *piste*. My first experience on skis was not a happy one and I imagined becoming the first person to climb Elbrus on crutches.

On 26 March, we were training in the Adsul Valley with a view to crossing the border into Georgia. Fatigue forced me to abandon this plan. On a down-hill, while heading back to our hotel, I was struggling not only to stay upright but also to avoid crashing into the pine trees which punctuated the snow-clad hillside.

Ahead, I could see four figures standing at the bottom of the hill. George slowed down. 'Say nothing, Pat. Absolutely nothing.'

As we drew closer, I could see they were soldiers, dressed in heavy greatcoats, each carrying an automatic machine gun. These lads looked business-like, not at all like the somewhat apathetic checkpoint guards we had encountered before now.

As usual, George began chatting in a friendly, relaxed manner. I just nodded my head where I thought it was appropriate to do so and adopted a silly grin.

The soldiers took a keen interest in our new Ski-Tour bindings, the likes of which they had not seen before. George was only too happy to give them an exhaustive demonstration. I did not understand one word which passed between the army patrol and my friend. George explained that we had left our papers back at the hotel, were humbly apologetic and would deliver ourselves and our papers to the barracks later that day if required to do so.

'You handled that well, George,' I said as we headed back towards Cheget. 'Were they not surprised by my silence?'

'No. I also told them you were not right in the head, but harmless.' And with that he sped off, laughing heartily.

Struggling to catch up, I generated more speed through the woods than was good for a person of my limited experience. George took a sharp turn to avoid a ditch in our path and I in turn attempted to follow his example on the tight bend. The path narrowed allowing me little room to manoeuvre. The turn was too demanding so I attempted to stop. One leg went broadside and snagged a tree while the other continued straight ahead.

My legs were wrenched in a most un-balletic configuration and searing pain shot from one knee to my groin. Like a string-less puppet, I struggled on my back to free myself from the skis as George continued on his way, oblivious to my plight.

Later that evening, I had a sauna and massage and felt a little better. Something had been damaged however, either a muscle or tendon, but I felt it was not serious enough to prevent my climb. The next day, we began our trek to the mountain. For the remainder of the expedition, the weather threw everything it could at us – blizzards, high gales and long periods of sunshine – but I was glad to be finally on the way to the summit.

With every step, stabs of pain radiated from my right knee but I fought to concentrate on something other than my discomfort. Once above the tree line, I became uncomfortably conscious of the change in temperature. It was positively icy. I had not felt this chilled even on the high exposed slopes of Everest and McKinley.

My decision to do a winter climb of Elbrus had been carefully considered. I knew that temperatures could plummet to below minus 40 degrees Celsius. I knew also that super-mountaineers like Reinhold Messner – who with Peter Habeler in 1978 climbed to the top of Everest without oxygen – had failed on his first attempt to climb this mountain in winter conditions.

In summer, Elbrus might not pose any great mountaineering challenge to the more experienced climber. However, in the winter months this was a mountain which offered little cake-walk opportunities. But never did I suspect that the extreme cold would cut so severely through to my thermal underclothing, having penetrated my down suit and polar fleece layers. At least the cold kept my mind off the knee injury.

A plan to construct a cable-car link from Azau Alm, 2,300 metres (7,475 feet), to the Pastuchov Rocks, 4,700 metres (15,2400 feet), which lie just south of Elbrus, has reached as far as Mir Station at 3,500 metres (11,500 feet).

The weather was so bad and George and I so affected by the cold, we decided to do what the vast majority of Elbrus climbers had done before us – take the cable-car to the terminus. From there, we would climb to the climbers' refuge known as the Prijut Hut at 4,200 metres (13,800 feet). Here we planned to spend the night and head off in the early morning for the west peak of this double-headed volcanic massif which we hoped to summit and retreat from in one day.

The cable-car dropped us at Mir and we slowly but progressively made our way to the Prijut shelter through deep snow and blinding white-out conditions. Three hours later, we came upon the refuge. Through the driving snow the hut looked like a giant aluminium-sided caravan.

This so-called 'Hut' can accommodate up to 200 people. It was constructed in 1938-'39 and is a three-storied, aluminium-clad building which has successfully resisted years of the harsh weather conditions characteristic of this mountain known as 'Little Antarctica'. It was razed by the Germans in the Second World War but re-built by the Russians.

Exhausted and bitterly cold, we were horrified to discover the Hut was locked – we had been told it would be left open for us. Left with no other choice, we made a forced entry to this building which, while dilapidated and without running water or electricity, was nonetheless a welcome retreat. This place was more like a deep-freeze meat store than a shelter for climbers. I spent that night dressed in my full down suit and wrapped in my sleeping bag and still shaking with the cold. The Hut had all the wind resistance of a string vest and icy draughts blew through it from all quarters.

At 2am, we rose, had a hot drink and something to eat and headed out into less than favourable conditions. Our objective was the West Peak, the highest point on the massif – 1.5 km distant and just 12 metres higher than its East Peak Siamese twin.

We trudged through deep snow north-east of the Hut heading for the Pastuchov Rocks at 4,700 metres (15,400 feet). Visibility was reduced by snow flurries and I longed for a clear view of the great mountain. No great climbing skill was required for this snow slope – but the threat of avalanche and crevasses was ever present.

By the time we reached the 'Rocks, the weather had worsened considerably. The bone-chilling wind increased in strength and drove us back to the Hut. We sat out the storm until 3am the following morning in that miserable place. On 29 March, we began our second attempt on the summit and prayed for a break in the weather.

Again, using compass and altimeter to find our way through an icy mist, we made a line for the Rocks. The mist became thicker and colder. Beyond the Pastuchov Rocks it was necessary for us to make a sweeping, arc-shaped traverse north-west and then north into the 5,325 metre (17,480 feet) saddle between the peaks.

This section was no dawdle and demanded precise navigation. We began the traverse and ended up in a field of crevasses. We found ourselves in a white-out as the weather closed in and the

190

risk here was much too great.

Back to the Hut for another cold, wretched night. This enormous ice giant I had chosen to conquer was not going to be an easy trophy. In fact, having been driven twice from this only recently dormant volcano, I was beginning to lose heart.

'What do you reckon, George?'

'There's no sign of a break in the weather. Let's go back down to the valley and relax for a day or two. We can then review the situation.'

I was glad to be getting back to a place where, while the night-time temperature was still well below freezing, conditions were less bitter. For the next two days we spent most of our time skiing. My right leg was still in pain but I soldiered on.

Fools' Day, 1 April, 1996 began with clear skies and warming sunshine. We packed our rucksacks and took the cable-car to the Mir Station. The snow on the lower reaches of the mountain had been hachured by the skis of the many people taking advantage of the fine weather. Taking our time and stopping frequently to watch the skiers, we eventually made the Prijut Hut. From here, we enjoyed the magnificent sight of the Caucasus Main Ridge and Elbrus' twin peaks reminded me of The Paps on the Cork-Kerry border. Unlike my beloved Irish hills, the scene before me was on a breathtaking scale. The circular lava massif, with a diameter of 18 km, stood nobly over the great icy wastes of these remote and exposed ramparts. People have perished of exposure even in summer in this place of high adventure. But on this day, the sunshine created a strikingly-bright allure which I had not witnessed before now.

At 2am on 2 April, we awoke, had breakfast and packed our rucksacks. Outside the draughty, high mountain hostel, the sky was an immense sheet of black velvet through which a myriad of pin-pricks of light escaped.

Two-and-a-half hours later, after a paced upward slog, we reached the Pastukhova Rocks.

'Let's hope it's third time lucky, George.'

Under the broad East Summit, we began our sickle-shaped sweep upwards. The strong winds had swept the recently-fallen snow from the mountain and conditions underfoot were icy and hard.

The dark morning silence was broken by the scraping of our

steel crampons biting each step into the steep slope. Shortly before 6am I felt I could no longer suffer the polar chill which was stinging my fingers and toes. A dread of frostbite, an affliction I was fortunate never to have experienced in my climbing career, almost forced me to retreat from the mountain.

'I don't know about you George but I've never felt so cold.'

'What you need Pat is a stiff vodka,' my climbing companion replied with a smirk.

'Okay – but I'll have mine without ice.'

As we proceeded slowly, I glanced at the sky above for the first rays of the rising sun.

By 6am, the slate-blue eastern sky was streaked with an orange-reddish hue as a new day's sun threw its honeyed light over the Caucasus. With the sun, my spirits rose, as did my body temperature, but only slightly. We had almost reached the saddle.

Standing in the cold cleavage of Elbrus' twin domes, five hours after leaving the Hut, we ate some chocolate and glanced ahead at the toughest part of the climb – almost four hours of undiluted, back-breaking toil. Slogging up the slope of hard ice became drudgery but every time I glanced above, the objective of this exercise drew nearer and a warm enthusiasm rushed through my veins. We spoke little. My chest heaved as my lungs sucked the thin air and chatting would have been a waste of energy and breath.

When we made it to the ridge leading to the summit, I paused to take in the remarkable views on all sides. The northern winter sun cast a low light across the motionless clouds far below us. Through breaks in this cover, I could see the frosted landscape. Everything was white, bright and glistening. A short jaunt across some icy rocks and we were standing on Europe's highest natural monument. It was 10.30am on 2 April, 1996 and I was elated beyond anything words could describe.

I gave my Russian friend a bear hug and he returned the gesture. We took the traditional summit photographs and stood there in silence for some moments feeling humbled by the majesty of these mountains.

'Are you ready to drop down, George?'

'Just a minute. I'm not ready yet.'

And with that George sat on his rucksack, produced his packet of cigarettes and lit one up. At 18,307 feet, the nicotine buzz must have been considerable. But nothing could have given me a greater high than the feeling of accomplishment. I had climbed five of the seven summits and Elbrus would be recorded as a winter ascent of which I was extremely proud. The pedantic would argue, of course, that the winter climbing season ends on the last day of March so I had not not scored a winter ascent – but, I was there and that was what it felt like.

The return journey was uneventful. We dropped from the crown of Elbrus with an eagerness prompted, in no small part, by the celebration we intended to have back at our hotel in Cheget.

During the climb, my single-minded determination to reach the top had banished all other thoughts. As soon as I reached the foot of the mountain, however, I was painfully reminded, in a sudden searing rush, of my leg injury. The pain would remain with me for weeks after my return home – a reminder that no mountain should ever be underestimated and of how close I came to failing my 'high five'.

Antarctica – Two to Go

If you can dream – and not make dreams your master
If you can think – and not make thoughts your aim;
If you can meet with Triumph and Disaster
And treat those two imposters just the same ...

Rudyard Kipling

'This can't be happening. These things are fuckin' useless. Man! I just don't believe this.'

Jeff Shea kept up his rant as I became more and more frustrated and hurt.

'Do you realise what this means? We're gonna have to fuckin' cancel the whole expedition. Where did you get these things anyway?'

The stove gave a last gasp, like the death throes of a landed fish, and the flame expired.

'Oh! We're fucked, man. That's it. It's all over. I've just thrown $20,000 down the toilet because you couldn't find stoves that work in these conditions.'

Shea was starting to annoy me, intensely, but there was nothing I could say. We were huddled in our tiny dome tent halfway up the highest point on the continent of Antarctica. The outside temperature was minus 40 degrees Celsius, inside it was not much better. Having climbed for seven hours on this, our first day on the Vinson Massif, we needed to take immediate and crucial measures to rehydrate our bodies. I had not slept in forty hours but the wonder of this place kept fatigue at bay.

It may be covered in snow and ice but the Antarctic is one of the driest environments on earth. A minimum of one gallon of water per person per day has to be consumed. If you're climbing in these conditions the liquid intake has to be considerably higher for survival. Our only means of replenishing our bodily requirements was to melt snow and stoves were probably the most important hardware items we carried on this ambitious and hazardous venture.

Jeff's whining was building to a cretinous crescendo. All I

194

wanted to do was tell him to 'shut fucking up!' but I couldn't. After all, I had planned this trip to the top of the bottom of the earth. I was the one who invited the team and organised the gear. I was the one who purchased the stoves – and the things did not work efficiently. His vitriolic outbursts would have been mine had the roles been reversed and while it is true that he buried deep under my skin for a time, I felt no real animosity towards Jeff. How could I? Here we were at the end of the earth having travelled many thousands of miles to follow a crazy dream and my little stoves, hissing and farting spent gas, controlled the success or otherwise of the odyssey.

'I spent a weekend in a meat freezer back home. These were tested to minus 30 degrees. What more could I do? Let's see if we can solve this problem.'

Again I ignited the burner on the white gas stove having cleared the jets of condensation before it froze solid. The pot of snow was placed atop as all eyes watched the clear blue flame. Within moments beads of condensation ran down the outer surface of the pot and began to douse the flame. It was as if the pot was full of pin holes as countless veins of moisture ran down the outer surface.

'Okay that's the problem. If we wipe away the condensation before it lands on the jets the stove should keep burning.'

Shea responded by hissing a sigh through clenched teeth just as the stove died again. Eventually, we established a motion of wiping, jet cleaning and re-igniting. It took us three times longer than should have been the case to melt a pot of snow but there was no way I was going to scupper this expedition, not yet.

This was to be the second last of my seven summits. My dream was looming ever larger on the horizon but the threat of it perishing in this strange land was becoming all too real. As I nursed the stove, my thoughts replayed the past year. Considering the difficulties I had faced in raising sponsorship for my continuing adventure, the last thing I would entertain was the thought of retreating from the Antarctic.

In the course of the seven summits challenge, I would dedicate over three years of my life to expeditions and training; travel some 200,000 kilometres, at times to some of the remotest corners of the earth, at a cost in excess of £70,000. Most of the money was raised through the diverse fundraising efforts of my support team at home. Had it not been for the enthusiastic response of my friends, sponsors and supporters – people who shared my dream with an intensity every bit as great as my own – I could never have planted a foot on any of the seven summits.

On 10 May, 1996, at the height of my sponsorship drive a sudden and furious storm high on the south side of Chomolungma caused the deaths of eight climbers. Among those killed were guide Rob Hall, a New Zealander who was leading a team when disaster struck, and Scott Fischer, a veteran guide from Seattle.

The tragedy, in terms of fatalities, was one of the single greatest mountaineering disasters ever. It fuelled the debate on whether or not too many adventurers were going where they did not belong. The sad incident also sent scurrying some potential corporate sponsors I had been wooing. For the next twelve weeks, I badgered my contacts in the media and orchestrated as much exposure on television, radio and the press as I could. It came to naught – there were some pledges of financial support but nothing firm. This did little for my resolve, considering the final leg of my adventure would be one of the costliest. The flight from Punta Arenas in Southern Chile to Patriot Hills, Antarctica would cost $17,000 alone and in the wake of Vinson Massif I intended to travel to Australia to climb Kosciusko, the seventh summit.

In the late summer of 1996, it looked as if I would have to put the rest of my adventure on hold. The cash was not there to meet the bookings I had already made with the various airlines. If something positive did not happen soon, I would have to break the bad news to the others, none of whom had the slightest suspicion of my impoverished state. I became a prisoner of hope, arriving each morning at my offices – from which I still ran an auctioneering and mortgage brokerage – and praying a letter or telephone call would arrive with the promise of a commercial patron.

On 5 August, while on my expedition in Africa with a group of 44 adventurers raising funds for the Irish charity Rehab, my office made contact with me and informed me of the contents of a letter that I received from the Mountaineering Council of Ireland (MCI). Inside was a covering note and a copy of a letter sent by an official in the Government's Department of Education to Michael Keyes, the then chairman of the MCI.

'I refer to your application for a grant in respect of the Seven Summits Challenge currently being undertaken by Mr Pat Falvey.

'I am pleased to inform you that the Minister for Sport, Mr Bernard Allen, TD has approved a grant of £20,000 towards the costs involved in completing the next stage of the challenge. This grant is being paid from the allocation to sport from the proceeds of the National Lottery and a payable order for £20,000 will issue shortly.'

The yelp I uttered on hearing this could have been heard all the way to the Minister's office in Dublin.

Many weeks earlier I had applied for support, via the MCI, to the Department of Education's Minister for Sport. In my application I outlined my intention to further develop my on-going programme of illustrated talks to school children throughout the country and expressed a willingness to further extend this educational dimension as the Minister saw fit. Minister Allen had responded with a generosity which left me nothing less than gobsmacked.

'I have a great story for you,' I said to one of my newsroom contacts in *The Examiner*. 'The Department of Education is giving me £20,000 towards the completion of the challenge.'

'You're not serious – twenty grand?' said the disbelieving reporter.

Next morning, the newspaper ran a story under the headline – 'Mountain Climber's £20,000 Leg-up For Completion Of Quest' and reported: 'One of this country's most ambitious sportsmen, and the first citizen of the Republic to climb Mount Everest, has received an unprecedented financial leg-up from the Department of Education to enable the realisation of a lofty goal ... Minister for Sport Bernard Allen said his Department had adopted a policy of support for sports which placed more emphasis on participation than competition ... Climbing, the Minister said, was one such activity which also took full advantage of "the great natural resources which are out there waiting to be enjoyed".'

Knowing that the MCI had received the £20,000 cheque from the department on my behalf, I awaited payment. In the meantime, I organised an overdraft facility with my bank and put my house as security to pay for the expedition. But it was not all plain sailing. Over the next few months some members of the MCI's executive committee became excessively officious towards me.

I knew by now there were certain individuals within the national climbing fraternity who were less than favourably disposed towards me. From early August, they held onto the grant money and at no time informed me of any difficulty. On 1 November, three months after receiving the cheque for £20,000, the MCI returned it to the Department of Education. That very day, I was on national radio thanking the National Lottery and the Department for their generous support.

This was a very embarrassing incident for me and put me under extra pressure to sort it out. Michael Keyes considered he ought to resign but was dissuaded. The MCI had previously agreed to administer the grant in a letter to the department. The bureaucratic paper storm of letters flying in every direction died down by the start of December and on 7 December 1996, just days before my departure, I received my grant. I was, at last, financially, physically and psychologically ready to climb the highest point on what has been called 'the last paradise on Earth' – the Antarctic.

As part of the final preparation, I spent 24 hours in a huge industrial meat freezer, which was about the size of a football pitch, testing the gear I would take to the most isolated and coldest continent. We set up home erecting two tents in the corner of this cold room. We christened this place 'little Antarctica', and tested the gear – tents, stoves, food, sleeping bags, boots and all the clothing we would be wearing. Nothing could be taken for granted in the godforsaken place that I was going to, 2,000 miles from civilisation. We would be camped on a 10,000-foot thick ice block in an area where no animal could survive and no plant would grow. The gear and equipment we were now testing would be to us the difference between survival and death. Equipment failure here could spell disaster. The national media took an enthusiastic interest in that particular experiment and this focus was 'warmly' welcomed by my freezer companions and best climbing buddies from Kerry – Con Moriarty, Gene Tangney and Mike O'Shea.

These three desperadoes had accepted my invitation to head down south and climb Mount Cook in New Zealand and Carstensz Pyramid in Irian Jaya – Indonesian New Guinea.

In minus 30 degrees Celsius we erected two tents in a corner of the cold store and bedded down for the night surrounded by thousands of tonnes of beef. While 'down under' I felt we might as well do a mountaineering sweep of the best mountains the southern hemisphere had to offer.

In between Mount Cook and Carstensz, the Kerry gang intended to accompany me to the final seventh summit. These were the people with whom I started my mountaineering adventures so it was especially poignant for me that they would be there to witness the last step to the summit of the last mountain.

As our first day in the meat freezer lengthened, the cold strengthened. When the last press reporters and photographers had left we took to our dome tents, in a corner of the cold store, buried ourselves in our sleeping bags and resisted the temptation to slip down to the nearest pub for a few pints in front of an open fire.

'What time is it, Falvey?'

'It's nearly midnight. Why? Have you a date? You couldn't get up to much in here. In fact, you probably couldn't get it up at all in this cold.'

'Did you say nearly twelve. Thank fuck! We couldn't get a pint now even if we wanted one – the pubs are closed.' And with that Gene Tangney finally settled down for the night.

The night was cold, not surprisingly, but not so much that we could not sleep. Early next morning, we sluggishly awoke and cooked breakfast on the stoves which never once gave any indication of the problems which would later arise on Vinson.

Shortly after breakfast, we were joined by national press, radio and TV reporters who had been following the progress of my expeditions. Pat Kenny, on his popular radio show, decided to conduct a live radio interview deep in the meat freezer. As a result, the 'Southern Hemisphere Expedition' aroused a lot of interest.

The ice had been broken, the funds were in place, and my passage to the Antarctic was clear. The time had come and I was on my way to complete the final stage of my dream.

On 5 January, 1997 I boarded a jet at Cork Airport which would carry me to Paris where I would rendezvous with my friend Thierry Reinard, a full-time mountaineer. Renard, in his early fifties, a small, wiry, super-fit adventurer had climbed with me on Everest in 1993. He would battle against Chomolungma three more times before finally summitting in 1996.

Along with Renard, the Antarctic team would include Jeff Shea, who worked in the computer business in San Francisco; Jean Luc Neidergang, a Frenchman who also worked in the computer sector and Dutchman Michael Jerjensen, a full-time adventurer. I had climbed before with Thierry, Jeff and Michael and knew these adventurers quite well. Jean Luc had climbed five of the seven summits and was heading for Everest after his polar enterprise.

Crackling with nervous energy and anticipation, we flew from Paris to Buenos Aires for a brief stop-over and then on to Punta Arenas in Southern Chile. This was to be our last contact with civilisation until we returned from Vinson.

Here, at the foot of the Chilean Andes on the western side of the Strait of Magellan, we had no intention of dawdling and wanted to get to the foot of the mountain as soon as possible. Mother Nature did not support our plans. For four days, we remained stranded as violent Antarctic storms lashed Patriot Hills. This was our last bus stop on the Vinson Massif excursion across Tierra del Fuego and the boiling South Atlantic, said to be a mariner's worst nightmare. We had chartered a huge Hercules C-130 transport plane to ferry us and our gear to Patriot Hills. It would also carry enough fuel not only for its return journey but to feed a light Cessna and a de Havilland Twin Otter which would fly our party from Patriot Hills to Base Camp.

We badgered the pilots a few times each day. But the message remained the same. 'Can't fly – weather is just too bad on the ice cap.'

Our time in Punta Arenas was spent sight-seeing. This very busy port attracts vessels from the South Atlantic fishery as well as research ships flying many flags.

The first European to visit this corner of the world was Ferdinand Magellan, who stopped off here in 1520. I was far more intrigued by the story told of Irish doctor, Thomas Fenton, who in the nineteenth century founded one of the largest and most prosperous sheep stations here. The success of his venture, and that of others who followed his lead, resulted in this part of Chile having a sheep population in excess of two million at the turn of the century.

In 1914, the Panama Canal was opened, resulting in a sharp decline in shipping around Cape Horn. Consequently Punta Arenas' importance as a port declined but a later oil boom kept the local economy well lubricated.

By the fourth day, we had visited practically every tourist attraction including the 'Jackass Penguin' colony about one hour northwest of the city. By now I felt that the plan to join my Kerry climbing friends on Mount Cook was starting to melt away.

Day five in Punta Arenas and our first duty was to call our carrier – Adventure Network International which has been ferrying climbers to the Vinson Massif each season since the mid-1980s.

'The storm has abated at Patriot Hills – we take off in two hours,' came the reply.

I immediately felt a rush of enthusiasm tinged with not a little nervousness. During my purgatorial stop-over in Punta Arenas I had learned that by far the greatest number of fatalities among expeditions arose as a result of flying mishaps.

Vinson, the highest point in the Sentinel Range, was discovered in 1958 by the US Air Force and named after Congressman Carl G Vinson of Georgia. The first ascent of the mountain was made on 17 December, 1966 by a private US team led by Nicholas B Clinch and sponsored by the American Alpine Club.

Adventure International Network – the company which was trucking us to our icy objective – has flown over 200 climbers to Vinson since 1985. But you need to have a proven track record of climbing in ice, snow and under extreme duress before they will consider taking you aboard.

'All aboard – next stop Patriot Hills!' declared our pilot after we had loaded the last of our gear and strapped ourselves to the seats on the floor of the huge cargo plane.

The unpretentious and functional Hercules was mostly loaded with fuel for its own journey and those of the Twin Otter and Cessna waiting for us at Patriot Hills to take us further into the

The Hercules plane felt like a tin can on the 2,000 km journey.

cold continent. Take-off on the concrete strip at Punta Arenas was uneventful but how could this four-engined monster land on ice? The deafening drone of the heavily burdened turbo-props resonated in every bone of my body but I was too pumped-up with adrenalin to be annoyed.

We flew over beech-blanketed lowlands, the open ranges of the vast sheep *estancias* and a myriad of deep fjords which reflected the sun's rays on their cold stainless-steel like surfaces. Eventually, we passed over the southernmost tip of Tierra del Fuego and above the boiling waters of the 'Furious Fifties' which have carved Cape Horn over the aeons.

To relieve the boredom of being down in the tin-can hold of the plane, we each took it in turns to spend time in the cockpit where three crew members flew while three others – who would fly on the return journey – slept.

Approaching the continental edge of Antarctica, I could see below me what at first my eyes told me were countless brilliant white sea gulls. These turned out to be a swarm of icebergs which had broken off the cap as the summer temperatures increased.

Flying over the white vastness of Antarctica, the reflected sun's light caught the plane in a halo of shimmering light. This, I felt, was as close as you could get on earth to the feeling of extra-terrestrial travel.

Less than eight hours later, the giant cargo plane began to nose down gradually as we made our approach to the natural, flat ice field at Patriot Hills in the Ellsworth Mountains, about 200 km from Mount Vinson. Looking out the windows of the cockpit, all I could see was a white, featureless canvas – it was impossible for me to tell how high we were above ground level but at least the pilots had gauges for that purpose. For a moment I thought I was travelling through another dimension – into what a child would imagine heaven to be like, a place of infinite whiteness.

The engines were throttled back with a monstrous roar, our air speed decreased and my hands gripped the arms of my seat. I could now make out the curvature of the earth below us. I felt an enormous shudder as the landing gear made contact. The giant plane briefly bounced back into the air and landed more heavily than the first time. The wheels rolled and skidded across the wind-grated, icy surface. No hydraulic brakes could be applied or the plane would go into an uncontrolled slide.

The pilot throttled back and forth in a bid to come to a slow and as steady a halt as was possible in these impossible conditions. It was the longest, noisiest landing I have ever experienced.

'Vinson here we come,' I yelped as we undid our seat belt buckles.

The rear door was dropped like an enormous steel jaw and my thoughts of a heavenly place were soon abandoned when a marrow-chilling breeze entered the cargo hold to remind us this was more an icy hell than a brilliant white heaven. Bracing polar air shifted feelings of flight lag from our senses as we unloaded the gear and fuel. This operation was carried out swiftly. The pilots had no intention of hanging around unnecessarily and were obviously anxious to fly back out, availing of the weather window which permitted access to this remote and strange land.

With a thunderous roar of the big engines, the Hercules turned and, blasting spindrift in all directions, ran along the vast ice field. It slowly rose into the azure sky and headed north to the nearest civilisation.

This was the austral summer but temperatures would never rise above minus 15 degrees Celsius and frequently dropped to minus 40 degrees during our stay.

Another concern was the notorious katabatic wind – caused by denser, colder air rushing from the polar plateau to the coast. These freeze-blasts could reach velocities of up to 320 km per hour. Everest may be a more physically demanding undertaking but the Antarctic puts man's frailty into shocking perspective.

Knowing we were quite some distance from the nearest settlement did not induce a feeling of isolation. How could it? Here, in the one place that can safely be called the 'middle of nowhere', is the only private semi-permanent camp on the continent. It offers accommodation for 50 people who can be 'housed' in large, insulated and heated tents. Cooking and kitchen facilities are laid-on and there's even a full-time medic.

Parked near the camp was a Twin Otter and Cessna – the planes which would carry us the 200 km to Vinson Base Camp. When the tourist/climbing season is over the tents, gear and even the Cessna are stored in a huge underground snow cave to be de-hibernated again when the winter darkness yields to the 20-hour daylight of summer.

In the mess tent, we feasted on a dinner of fresh meat, vegetables and dessert in the company of people who were making the journey to the Pole. Many of these were middle-aged and well-heeled, people who could not wait to get home to their coffee mornings and dinner parties and tell of their exploits at the South Pole. And as we say in Ireland – 'fair play to them.'

A 65-year old American lady, who sat beside me at the dinner table, said for 45 years it had been her ambition to stand on the South Pole for reasons which she could not fully rationalise. While telling her of my successful ascent of Everest, I detected a glint in her friendly eyes. 'Well, if you want to climb Everest don't wait another 45 years,' I joked as I excused myself from the table.

Outside, I stood looking at the extraordinary vastness of it all – in some directions it was impossible to tell where the land ended and the sky began. Everything was illusionary. Hills in the distance could either have been as small as the Kerry mountains or as enormous as some Himalayan monoliths. There was no way of telling. Scale had no application in this place.

The small Cessna which flew us from Patriot Hills to Base Camp. Mount Vinson is in the background.

After ten hours waiting at Patriot Hills while we waited for the wind to abate at base camp we packed our gear and ourselves intothe Ski equipped Twin Otter and the Cessna and headed for the top of the bottom of the world. Shoe-horned into the small plane I was lucky to get a window seat. The white expanse below looked like a huge, seamless, plain of cloud. Then, almost unexpectedly, the virgin canvass was penetrated by the white peaks of the mountain range.

We landed on the Branscombe Glacier at an altitude of 2,308 metres (7,500 feet). I jumped from the cramped plane onto the shallow snow. Speechless, I stood transfixed by the beauty of this place. The giant glacier flowed through a narrow valley above which there was a spectacular icefall and above and behind that was Vinson itself. We had no sooner landed on the glacier then we received a weather alert.

'Okay lads, here's the latest forecast. There's a weather system moving in on Vinson. It will come in at 3,000 feet in 48 hours and move to 10,000 over the next few days. If we go now we should be able to outrun it to a higher altitude.'

The team agreed to go immediately and move higher up the mountain. We sorted out our gear and loaded our sleds and rucksacks straight from the plane. We decided to rest for an hour and go for it. We had not slept in over 40 hours but everybody was so fired-up with enthusiasm, exhaustion never got a look-in.

It was now 3am in the land of the midnight sun as we put on our skis and rucksacks and attached our sleds to our harness, each one of us carrying over 100kg of gear. 'Okay lads, let's go for it – we've already lost four days because of weather,' I uttered and with that we skied our way up the gradual, hard ice hill to Camp One at 2,769 metres (9,000 feet). The effort of pulling our heavy sleds had us bent over like a string of old men walking in a head wind.

Seven hours of this monotonous slog and I was glad to reach Camp One where pitching our two dome tents was an unpleasant experience. The effort of erecting the tents was not as great as that which was required for the long, slow plod from Base Camp and our bodies began to feel the chill far more acutely. Huddled in the tents, at last, the stoves were fired-up – more than once, unfortunately. We drank a concentrated carbohydrate soup which took longer to prepare than our patience would allow.

'We can't continue with these fucking things – they are no fucking good,' exclaimed Jeff.

'These are MSR stoves – same as those used by Reinhold Messner and Arved Fuchs when they did their 2,800 km trek across Antarctica in 1990,' I said, hoping this would quell the diatribe.

'I'd believe that. They must be the very same stoves – that would explain why they're konked-out.'

We were tired now so we decided to get some rest first and things might be better after a few hours sleep. The following day, as we left camp, after a period of fitful, cold sleep, I stopped on the glacier to look below. Sure enough, on the horizon was the dark cloud formation of the incoming storm. The tempest looked like dust rising above some supernatural posse on our trail.

'How fast is that storm moving?'

'I don't know, Pat. But it's closing on us. What if it goes above 10,000 feet? What will happen then?'

'*Sacre bleu!* Don't even think about that Thierry. Let's mush up this mountain a bit further and make camp.'

The day-long trek to Camp Two at 3,100 metres was a cold carbon copy of the ski-shuffle the previous day. We radioed Patriot Hills again for a forecast and were advised to get high as fast as we could. The weather front was still on our tails.

The following day, after a good night's sleep, our fourth day on the mountain began early. We abandoned our sleds and carried, on our backs, all we would need to make it to the summit and back to Camp Three.

With our sleds, we left behind a cache of supplies. If the storm, which was chasing our tails, decided to dump on us, these would be our only hope of survival in this place.

We made our way through what is known as the icefall, dodging some interesting crevasses as we climbed to our high camp at 3,692 metres (12,000 feet) where we set up Camp Three in the exposed saddle between Mount Shinn and Vinson. This was an amazing place to be camped. We were now sitting on top of a storm in minus 20 degrees Celsius – clear, bright weather with pristine blue skies and the ultra violet rays of the sun beating down on our sunburnt bodies.

We pitched our tents, taking extra precautions to put further protection around the perimeters in the event that the storm that lay 1,000 feet below would rise and engulf us. We prepared for a long confinement. Once we were sure that our home on this 12,000 foot thick block of ice was secure, we retired for the night to the warmth of our sleeping bags to cook a meal and make a decision on the next course of action.

Once again we radioed Patriot Hill for a forecast. Their reading was that the storm would blow itself out and would not rise any higher. Our plan was revised once again and our decision was to go for the summit in twelve hours depending on the movement of the incoming stormy weather. At this stage my upper legs and back ached from dragging the 60 kg sled. Each member of the team was tired and cold – damn cold.

'Tomorrow we race to the top and hope the storm crashes out below us at 10,000 feet,' I said with feigned optimism, realising that the mountain now looked as if it was emerging through the surface of a gurgling cauldron.

Day five dawned, in as much as it can when you have 24 hours daylight. We exited our tents at minus 30 degrees Celsius to check what the day had in store. The cloud storms below were holding and the day above looked good. After a little discussion we made a team decision to go for it. In the early morning cool we headed off up the final section of our climb to the top of the most beautiful and remote continent in the world.

We had not used our skis since leaving Camp Two. Out came the crampons again. After the first few yards, I was amazed how difficult it was to dig the steel points into the ice. The ground was as hard as high tensile steel under what was never more than a thin dusting of spindrift. We roped together into a team of three and two in the event of falling into one of the many crevasses en route. After five freezing hours scratching our way up a seemingly end-less chute we made it to the final 1,000 feet – the summit ridge.

Roped together, we struggled against the thin air. It was diffi-cult for everybody to move at the same pace. Muscles were weary, joints were over-taxed but the sight of the summit drew us on like moths to a candle-light.

Near the top, patience thinned out with the air. Any time one of the rear climbers lost pace and created resistance on the rope, the tug would be met with a barrage of expletives from the front-run-ners. This was a sure sign that exhaustion was setting in but the storm clouds, still bubbling up the mountain below us, were all the added incentive we needed to continue onwards and upwards.

Jean Luc found it exceptionally hard going but none of us was less than seriously exhausted. On this final leg Jeff almost sparked-off a violent mutiny when he declared, for reasons which were never fully explained, that we were on the wrong mountain.

'No, it's that mountain over there – that's Vinson,' he declared, with arrogance more than confidence, and pointing to a nearby peak. He stopped, refusing to go any further. 'What's the point? This is not Vinson. We should be on that mountain over there.'

For the first time temperatures rose and blood boiled as we struggled, using maps and compass, to explain he was wrong. Reluctantly, he came about and continued onwards and upwards.

I had climbed many more technically demanding and higher mountains but never in my life had I ever felt such physically torturous cold. My toes and fingers were numb and I feared frostbite was beginning to take its toll. After every few paces, I stamped my feet on the unyielding frozen surface of the mountain and slapped my hands together in a desperate bid to keep the circulation going. I was worried – the polar chill was burning up my energy at an enormous rate.

'Nearly there. Nearly there. Come on Pat – you can do it. Come on,' a voice kept saying in my head like a mantra.

One hour's climbing on the summit ridge and we were approaching the summit cornice. There was no fear of avalanche here where the snow was as hard as granite.

I was glad of the neoprene mask which helped take some chill out of the air being inhaled and prevented exhaled air condensing and freezing on my face. On this totally exposed monument, I resolutely climbed upwards, keeping my sights firmly fixed on the top.

On 24 January 1997, I took the final steps to the top of the most magnificent, unspoiled and, perhaps, loneliest place on earth. Proud to be an Irishman to climb Mount Vinson, my thoughts turned to the early explorers whose bravery and determination compensated for the shortcomings of their far less sophisticated equipment. The longer I spent in Antarctica, the greater my respect for the early pioneers became. My thoughts turned especially to Ernest Shackleton and Kerryman, Tom Crean, who served as his second officer on the *Endurance* which was crushed by the polar ice. The sinking, at the turn of the century, led to an incredible 600-mile trek across ice and ocean to Elephant Island and from there an equally inconceivable 700-mile open boat journey to South Georgia where Shackleton and his brave comrades crossed the uncharted mountains of the island.

Thierry took a photograph of me hoisting my country's Tricolour above Antarctica.

'Just a sec – there's one more photograph you must take.'

I rummaged in my rucksack and found what I was looking for. 'What is that?'

'This is Jack, the sixth member of the team. He's the quiet one,' I said as I held a leopard seal soft toy in my arms. The toy had been given to me by the boys and girls at a small primary school at Clogagh, near Bandon in County Cork. There were two seals – one called Jack and the other, predictably enough, Jill. The children asked me to take Jack with me as a lucky charm and on my return from the final seven summits climb, visit the school once more and reunite the pair.

'Right, back in the pack Jack, it's time to head for Australia.'

Before I left the summit of Mount Vinson, I stood quietly for a few seconds looking at the view, the likes of which I had never witnessed. On all sides the white vastness stretched to the edge of the earth where the deep blue sky faded to white at the cusp. This expansive sea of brilliant white snow and ice was broken by what appeared to be widely-scattered archipelagos. These were the great mountains of the Antarctic, few of which have been climbed but none were higher than the ground on which I now stood.

'You did it boy, you fucking did it,' I told myself as I headed back down to Base Camp.

The storm, which had been nibbling at our backsides for the duration of the climb, had abated against the mountain further down and was no longer any threat.

As soon as we returned to our high camp we radioed Patriot Hills seeking the latest forecast and it was less than promising. Another squall was heading this way. If we got to Base Camp in the next day and a half we could be airlifted to Patriot Hills. We could then radio to the pilots of the Hercules who were waiting for a call in Chile over 2,000 km away to come and collect us.

At our high camp we ate, drank and after a restful sleep we made our way to Base Camp. The following morning, we were back to work and pushing ourselves to our physical limits. We slogged for over fourteen hours on a rapid descent to Base Camp.

On arrival, my energy levels were very low as we erected our tents. I was freezing to the core in the Antarctic cold even though I had my minus 40 degree one piece down suit on. I crawled into my sleeping bag, fully clothed and feeling tired, miserable and constantly cold.

Then it started. The sun was behind the mountains and there was little heat in the tents. Suddenly, every muscle in my body went into spasm. I was being jerked violently and uncontrollably. I had no idea what was wrong. My thoughts, in any case, were now focused on just one single objective – to stay alive. For five hours, I lay in this violently shivering state. My speech was slurred and my extremities numb. Jean Luc and Jeff gave me copious warm drinks and huddled close to share their body heat.

When the sun emerged from behind the mountains and hit the wall of the tent, the inner temperature rose a few degrees and as it did, my muscles slowly began to relax. 'Thank you dear God,' I thought, 'I'm not going to die.'

I boarded the Cessna that day feeling drained of all energy. As well as carrying extraordinary memories of the adventure we took with us bags of waste, including our urine and excrement, making sure the only thing we left on Vinson were our footprints.

Back at Patriot Hills, the medic explained that my body had lost heat faster than it could produce it. This is called hypothermia – it is often fatal and I was lucky to be alive.

'I suggest you take plenty of rest when you get back to Punta Arenas, Pat. Take it easy for a while.'

'I'm afraid I can't stay long in Chile – I've an appointment to meet some friends on Mount Cook.'

'Are you crazy?'

He was not the first person to ask that question, and I knew he would not be the last.

On saying my farewell to Antarctica, I was resolved to come again some day.

SEVEN UP

An Everest mountaineer's burning ambition to climb the seven highest peaks on the seven continents of the earth may include more expeditions than he originally planned.
By the time Pat Falvey has finally added his name to an exclusive 'club' of Seven Summit climbers he may have scaled not seven mountains, but nine.

The article in *The Examiner* newspaper which appeared towards the end of December, 1996 – shortly before my departure for Antarctica – went on to explain a geographical quandary which I found myself grappling with. Prior to that, my knowledge of plate tectonics was as vague as my understanding of quantum physics. Now, however, I was studying books and articles explaining the natural phenomenon of floating continents.

After much careful consideration my final plan was to climb Mount Kosciusko 2,228 metres (7,310 feet) situated in the unimaginatively-labelled Snowy Mountains of the Australian Alps. This minor mountain was widely regarded as the traditional 'seventh' summit, depending, of course, in which order the peaks were climbed. Some would argue that Carstensz Pyramid, 5,076 metres (16,650 feet), in Irian Jaya – Indonesian New Guinea – qualified as the last. Carstensz had all the allure of a classic expedition and I was very drawn to the idea of meeting some of the colourful tribes of the region.

Yet another school of thought favoured Mount Cook in New Zealand, 3,846 metres (12,620 feet) as the 'true' seventh. Before confusion made his masterpiece, I turned to the writings of Glenn Porzak, past president of the American Alpine Club, who had climbed the Carstensz Pyramid as well as the other seven summits and who stated – 'technicalities, politics and philosophy aside, two facts stand out. New Guinea is an island and Carstensz is the highest mountain in the world situated on an island. Therefore, Kosicusko is the seventh summit. As the highest mountain in the world not located on a continent, Carstensz is surely the eighth.' And because these areas fascinated and intrigued me, I would add

211

Mount Cook in New Zealand.

them to my Southern Hemisphere expedition.

I invited three of my best friends, Con Moriarty, Mike Shea and Gene Tangney to accompany me on this 45,000 km expedition to Australia, New Zealand and Irian Jaya.

My arrival at the foot of Mount Cook had been delayed by the weather I had experienced during the expedition to Antarctica. The intense and earnest desire to meet up with my three friends banished any fatigue I may have suffered in the wake of the Vinson climb.

On the morning of 1 February, 1997, I was making my way to the Plateau Hut, 2,242 metres (7,335 feet), a popular climbers' base for those taking some of the more classic routes to the summits of Cook and Tasman. In the middle distance, against a snow-covered backdrop, I could clearly see some figures dressed in bright yellow and black jackets, just like the ones donated to the lads by a sponsor, Vaude, back home. As I drew closer there was no mistaking Con's big silhouette against the mountain.

'Jesus! It's Falvey.' And with that they descended upon me in a shower of hugging and back-slapping.

'Well, how did it go?'

'I made it. It was brilliant. The place was amazing. I've never been anywhere like it before.'

'Any complications?' asked Con, hungry for a detailed, step-by-step account of the trek to the top of the Antarctic. The next few hours were spent recounting my exploits and learning from the lads of the unfolding events of the mountain. Con and Gene had just returned from climbing the classic North Ridge of Mount Cook as I arrived and they were also as high as kites. They had feared that due to my delay in Antarctica I wasn't coming, and that, as the weather was good they took the opportunity to go for an alternative route to that which we had planned – the East Ridge traverse of the mountain.

'This calls for a drink – Pat, did you bring any ice?' joked Gene Tangney as the rucksacks were enthusiastically rummaged for some celebratory tincture.

The following day the weather broke for the worst and we all took time off at Mount Cook Base Camp in the company of two other climbers – Brian Galvin, originally from Beaufort in Kerry but living in Australia, and Dingle man, Mick Quirke. Most of the day was spent discussing our next strategy for our expedition on the mountain. As soon as the weather would clear, Mike Shea and I would attempt the classical Linda Glacier with Mike Quirke and Brian Galvin and when we'd return, Con, Gene, Mike and I, together, would attempt the more difficult East Ridge.

Filled with the joy of being back on a great mountain with some of my closest friends, I was in no way vexed by the bad weather which pinned us down for three days. It was also giving me a chance to recover from my exploits in Antarctica.

This tent-shaped mountain, known to the native Maori as the god Aoraki, was first climbed on Christmas Day, 1894, by local mountain men Jack Clarke, Tom Fyfe and George Graham.

Edmund Hillary honed his climbing skills on this mountain which, despite its stunning almost Himalayan aura, is a killer – five climbers per annum is the average death toll. Inexperience is the commonest cause of fatality but being only 44 kilometres from the weather kitchen of the Tasman coast, Cook can undergo extreme climate changes with great speed. These vagaries of weather can play havoc with the most experienced expeditions on this mountain which has special and historical significance for Irish climbers.

In 1882 an Irish vicar, William Green, made the slow and lengthy sea, train and horse-back journey from his home to New Zealand. In the company of two Swiss companions, Emile Boss and Ulrich Kaufmann, these intrepid adventurers made it to the Linda Glacier high on Mount Cook. With night falling and a northwesterly storm racing towards the mountain the party turned back when only 50 metres from the summit.

Successfully taking on the challenge of a great mountain is not always about leaving your footprints on the topmost point. It is more about experiencing your body's physical and mental capabilities when pitted against the extremes of a harsh environment and learning from that game of taking calculated risks.

William Green's achievement was considerable, especially in an age which pre-dated fast and relatively stress-less modes of modern transportation and the emergence of high-tech climbing boots, clothing and equipment.

It was his memory I carried with me to the summit of Cook, which we climbed after some exciting snow and ice climbing along the Linda Glacier route.

Crossing the heavily crevassed lower reaches of the glacier we remained ever conscious of the appalling avalanche reputation this section of the mountain had earned, at considerable human cost, over the years. Without discussing it openly, we all thought also of the Mount Cook rock avalanche on 14 December, 1991, when an almost incomprehensible 14 million cubic metres of a rock buttress on the east face fell away and roared 2,720 metres down the mountain. The mass of debris travelling down the 57-degrees slope reached speeds which touched 600 kilometres per hour. The debris flowed out across the crevassed area down the Grand Plateau to the head of the Hochstetter Icefall and over the surrounding glaciers for 7.3 kilometres. An accompanying dust cloud rose 700 metres up the side of the Malte Brun Range and the air blast was felt 5 kilometres away. Mount Cook was reduced in height by about 20 metres as a result of this display of dominion by the god Aoraki.

After returning from the summit, we received a weather forecast that more bad weather was on its way which put our objective of climbing the East Ridge out of reach in the time we'd have left. We decided, rather than waste time on the glacier, we'd evacuate the mountain and go to lower altitudes where the weather would be better. From Mount Cook village we travelled to the famous Fiordland National Park, home of the world-famous Milford Sound, Mitre Peak and the Sunderland Falls (one of the highest waterfalls in the world). While there, we enjoyed the privilege of an exciting climb on one of the country's best known mountains,

Mitre Peak, a Matterhorn-like mountain that shoots to over 6,000 feet to the sky directly from the sea. After descending this beautiful peak, we prepared for the next part of our journey.

My memories of New Zealand are of long and oddly relaxing hours spent ice and snow climbing in the company of good friends. We claimed the highest ground without incident and, from the time we made it back to Base Camp, I could sense the build-up of some great *craic* with the imminent fulfilment of my dream.

Leaving New Zealand behind us, we flew to Sydney where some days were spent soaking up the atmosphere with other tourists. I found this all too western and felt a strong urge to

Gene and Pat at Milford Sound, New Zealand, before climbing Mitre Peak.

knock in a manner of speaking, Kosciusko so that I could then make tracks towards Irian Jaya and escape into what by all accounts was still very much a 'land before time'.

We cut short our visit to Sydney and hired a car to make the long drive to the Snowy Mountains.

Among the provisions we packed for this odyssey or, as Con was wont to say – 'odyssey me bollocks!' – were some bottles of the best supermarket champagne we could find.

Along the road we joked, sang, dozed, shared the driving and I felt that it was just like old times – the same bunch of friends heading off on just another trip to the mountains.

Deep in my heart, I remained conscious of the fact that this was not just another climbing exploit. After many years of dreaming, planning, fundraising, fretting, risk-taking – and, on occasion, being more single-minded than was fair to those close to me – I was about to step from dreamland into the bright, sharp light of reality.

The undertaking, which subconsciously began with that very first walk in the Kerry hills with my good friend Val Deane, gave my life a focus and a tremendous sense of purpose. Along the way I made many valued friends, experienced the struggle of life in far-away lands and marvelled at the awesome beauty and ferocity of nature. There were times when I felt physically and emotionally sick and tired and questioned the logic of situations like spending long hours of confinement in a small, cold, smelly tent wondering if the next gust of snow-laden wind would blow me into the next life. But the pleasures far outweighed the pains. The warmth of the welcomes after each expedition, the genuine devotion of my family and friends, the unselfish and unflinching support of my climbing and mountain walking colleagues fuelled my spirit and fed my determination.

'Jaysus Falvey, you're looking very pensive,' said Gene Tangney glancing in the rear-view mirror of the car.

We were on the approach to Lake Gindabyne, some 400 kilometres from Canberra and our starting-point for the climb to Kosciusko – a mountain which has suffered the ignominy of having a post box, and road, planted near its summit.

Gene was behind the wheel and I was in the back seat staring at the sky-line just above the horizon.

'No, I'm not pensive. Well, maybe a little. I was just thinking of the great times we've had.'

'You make it sound as if we're all used-up.'

'You look fairly used-up Tangney.'

'So would you if you had been driving for the past four hours.'

'I'm the VIP, the star of the show. I'm saving my energy for the final seventh – the realisation of the dream, the completion of the odyssey.'

'Oh! Not the fuckin' odyssey again,' said a growling Con. 'You're not Homer, you know.'

'Who are you calling a homo?'

'I said Homer, not homo.'

'Oh! Homer Simpson.'

'Tangney, stop the car, I'm getting out,' threatened Con. 'Homo – Jaysus, do you know anything Falvey?'

'I know how to dream. "All men dream: but not equally. Those who dream by night in the dusty recesses of their minds wake in the day to find that it was vanity ..."'

216

'Stop the fuckin' car, Tangney. I can't take it any more.'

'"... but the dreamers of the day are dangerous men, for they may act their dreams with open eyes, to make it possible." Ah! good ol' T E Lawrence. Tell me Con, did you ever see any of his films?'

'Who?'

'Lawrence.'

'Lawrence of Arabia?'

'No. Lawrence and Hardy."

'Stop the *caaaar!*'

Heavy almost viscid raindrops began to dot the windscreen as we approached the mountain which Con jokingly called 'the pimple'. Pulling up outside our lodgings the rain began to increase in intensity. By the time we had unpacked the car it had deteriorated into a deluge of almost biblical proportions. Our intention was to climb Kosciusko on the day of our arrival and put our Irian Jaya plan in train. It was as if some force greater than our combined dynamism was saying – 'you might be ready, but I'm not ready to let you.'

The following morning dawned slightly brighter than that of the previous day. After breakfast, we relaxed and resisted the temptation to take to the trail and put the seventh in the bag. The climb to the 2,230 metres (7,310 feet) summit would be undertaken that evening. I had agreed to link-up by satellite telephone to the Pat Kenny radio show on RTE once I had achieved my goal. Because of the time difference between Ireland and New South Wales it had to be late in the day before I could stand atop Australia.

The hours dragged on but at least the rain didn't. And that evening we trudged through muddy ground along the well-worn path. We could have been heading up the Macgillycuddy's Reeks in County Kerry. The fading evening light cast its dim glow over the blankets of mountain grasses lying each side of the trail. A diffused glow emanated from the surface of the many tarns which had been swelled to overflowing by the recent rains.

'It's like being back home, lads.'

'Yeah! Even the rain was the same.'

The chatter of some Australian acquaintances, who had decided to accompany us, was the only tangible reminder of exactly where we were. Our conversation along the easy walk had been so

In the dark, on the summit of Kosciusko.

nonstop that it was almost with abruptness we reached the gentle point of the summit.

'*Comhghairdeachs, maith an fear!* ... Congratulations, Pat. ... Well done! ...'

One by one, my friends shook my hand and hugged me as I stood there in the late evening darkness. Tears welled in my eyes as a whole gamut of emotions stampeded through my mind. Feelings of pride, joy and happiness were tinged with sadness. Some brave men and women I had met along the way to the seven summits had died. I would miss their company but their spirit would be with me any time I planted my feet on a mountain. Their spirit was with me now as I glanced at the smiling faces of my friends caught in the beams of the torches here at the end of my voyage of discovery. Con dialled the number of the radio station back home in Ireland, made the connection and handed me the cellular telephone.

'Congratulations, Pat. You have climbed the seven highest mountains on the seven continents. You completed this remarkable feat on today, 14 February. How do you feel?'

'Well, I feel absolutely on a high. My dream is now a reality.' And, shining my torch light into the bearded face of Con Moriarty, I continued – 'Finally, the odyssey has ended, but I'm just beginning.'

218

What's Next?

*I am no mountaineer in the strict sense. Mountains, strongly as they
have always attracted me, are not for me aims in themselves, tests of
technical accomplishment and physical strength; they are only part of
that great world in which I feel so much at home. I love mountain peaks
as I love people, because they are equivalent parts of a greater whole.*

Herbert Tichy

'Take care lads, say hi to all at home and give everyone my love.'

I sadly bid farewell to Con, Gene and Mike. They were home-
ward bound for Ireland from a small airport in Wamena, a modern
town in the beautiful Baliem valley. It is a fascinating place situated in the centre of many miles of vast jungle and rainforest in
Indonesian-controlled Irian Jaya (New Guinea). We had decided to
end our attempt to climb the Carstensz Pyramid. After two weeks
living and trekking in the rain forests the risks to the lives of our
porters and ourselves were too great. We were in the area without
a permit and had to dodge the government soldiers and military
convoys. These troops were trying to suppress the outlawed resistance movement, the OPM (Organisasi Papua Merdeka) or Free
Papua Movement. It seems that these poor freedom fighters are
fighting a losing battle with bows and arrows and a handful of
guns as they try to resist the Indonesian annexation of West New
Guinea.

The government of Indonesia has set its sights on the vast natural resources of this province and has set a policy of exploiting
these for their own benefit having little regard for the people living
there. Our stay with the indigenous people of the area gave us a
better insight into the current problems faced by them and the
injustices which they have to put up with as they look for equality,
freedom and the right to promote their traditions and cultures.
They are also trying to protect the rainforest and their natural
resources – 'their homes'. Most are frustrated as they feel that you
are destined to fail against the might of the Indonesian military
machine.

However, the peace and tranquillity I found there, with a people who until recently were warriors and cannibals, intrigued me. For the first time in months, I felt completely relaxed on my own. I decided I needed to take time out.

After the lads flew off I headed off for a week into a nearby village with my friend Justinus J. Darby. I had become acquainted with Justinus while on our short stay in Wamena. I had the privilege of being invited to stay with him and his people in their village – how could I refuse such an opportunity? It would give me the chance I needed to reflect on my future before I'd return to the restrictions and hassle of my modern day life and where better to contemplate this than here in the garden of paradise.

There were lots of simple questions I had to ask myself, some of which I had ignored for far too long. The reality of life was about to dawn on me when I'd return to Ireland. How was I going to make a living? What do I want to do next? What direction was my life taking? My head was full of new ideas, dreams and aspirations. It was time now once again to refocus on new ambitions.

After a relaxing week among these simple, intelligent people, I was ready emotionally and physically for my return journey to Ireland. I bid my farewell to Justinus and his family and was delighted to be heading home, content with my achievements and ready to concentrate on the next phase of my life.

On landing at Cork Airport, I was ecstatic to be welcomed home by Minister Hugh Coveney on behalf of the government and the Lord Mayor, Councillor Jim Corr. There was also a large gathering of my family, loyal supporters and the media. The people there had encouraged and been with me from the start of my odyssey of adventure and exploration to the seven continents of the world.

At a press conference, the first question to be asked was obvious: 'Well Pat, what's next?'

APPENDIX

CAMERAS USED

Cannon EOS 100
Pentax 105

FILM USED

Fugi 100 slide film

Video Cameras Used

Sony 3 Clip Digital
Sony Hi 8 Handycam